Breathing the Psalms

*Praying the Psalms
One Breath at a Time*

BILL RANDALL

Breathing the Psalms: Praying the Psalms One Breath at a Time

© 2025 Bill Randall

ISBN-13: 979-8-9993767-0-1
First edition: August 2025
Cover design by *100 Covers*

All rights reserved. No portion of this book may be reproduced, stored in a retrieval system, or transmitted in any form or by any means—electronic, mechanical, photocopy, recording, scanning, or other—except for brief quotations in critical reviews or articles, without the prior written permission of the publisher.

Scripture quotations are taken from the Holy Bible, New International Version®, NIV®. Copyright © 1973, 1978, 1984, 2011 by Biblica, Inc.® Used by permission of Zondervan. All rights reserved worldwide. www.Zondervan.com. The "NIV" and "New International Version" are trademarks registered in the United States Patent and Trademark Office by Biblica, Inc.

The breath prayers inspired by passages from the Psalms are often an adaptation of the biblical text.

www.longwake.com

Lasting influence flows from the integration of who we are and what we do as followers of Jesus under the influence of the Holy Spirit. Long Wake Publishing produces resources committed to both.

DEDICATION

The Novo Mission Lead Team:

Mark Thrash, Darren Prince, Chris Somogyi, Matt Weston, Kevin Brown, Lee Price, Chris Marshall, and Jill Randall, my wife and partner in ministry.

It is a joy and privilege to serve Jesus and the advancement of his Kingdom with you.

ACKNOWLEDGEMENTS

I extend my heartfelt thanks to Ruth Happ for her practical support throughout this writing project.

I'm also deeply grateful to Darren Prince, my thought-leader buddy. Our many years of delving into scripture and exploring other great books together have been both enlightening and fun—I look forward to many more shared experiences with you.

Finally, my deepest appreciation goes to my amazing bride and partner in all things, Jill. Your unwavering encouragement and invaluable feedback have been a constant source of strength. I truly would not be the man I am today without you.

CONTENTS

Foreword	1
Introduction	3
The Difference Between Christian and Eastern Meditation Practices	4
A Practice Both Ancient and Relevant	5
How to Use This Book	6
Praying the Psalms One Breath at a Time	9
About the Author	161

FOREWORD

A few months back, I came to a dead end in my daily devotional reading. Ever the high-achiever, I would secretly pride myself on the numerous Bible plans I had completed. Daily devotions were dialed in, reading plans on lock, each chapter flying by as fast as I could check the box.

That's when the still, small voice of the Risen King broke through my routine to gently invite me deeper. How kind of him to say it this way, "Darren, when you read the written Word, are you meeting with me, or are you meeting a goal?"

Ouch.

But . . . wow.

Dr. Bill Randall has set a table here for stopping the treadmill of our daily devotions to slow down, go deeper, and truly encounter Jesus. Breath prayer, including a meditative reading of scripture accompanied by listening to the whispers of the Spirit, is not a new idea. Bill will be the first to tell you that there is nothing new under the sun.

And yet, there is something new here. Bill takes us from text to prayer to listening and then to the key ingredient, a declaration of action that calls us to respond in obedience. Most devotional writing will script that out for you, almost like you're getting to eavesdrop on a conversation that doesn't involve you. Not here. This is written in gentle humility by one seasoned enough in praying the Psalms to know that the best "I will" statements can't be set down in ink as one-size-fits all. There's a humble trust on these pages that Jesus himself will issue a personal *rhema*-word for every reader. How grateful I am for an author who will decrease enough for the voice of Jesus to increase and call me to daily obedience!

My scuba-diving friends (of whom I am absolutely not considered an insider) tell me that the only safe way to return to the surface after a sustained deep dive is by slowing one's ascent. The pressure at great depth is too much to rapidly resurface without pausing to adjust, breathing at increments along the way. Resurface too soon, and your body won't respond well to a hasty arrival at sea level.

Breath prayer is a depth of scripture meditation that takes us deep below the surface of the soul. The waters can be dark and murky, but they are also alive with shapes and colors never-before-seen at the surface level. Listening prayer hoists us back up at a sustainable pace. Crafting an "I will statement" in response adjusts our lungs back to life on the surface level, enabling us to thrive in the choppy waters of these days we live in.

I'm so grateful for this daily rhythm of diving deep into a Psalm, breathing in a simple phrase at the depths, and then resurfacing for a life of obedience.

And I'm so grateful for Bill's gracious invitation to explore the depths in a way that leads to truth, to life, to action. May you meet with Jesus rather than meet a goal on these pages ahead!

Darren Prince
Executive Vice President, Novo Mission
London, England
April, 2025

INTRODUCTION

Nobody ever told me that prayer could be like breathing!

Like many, I deeply love God and his incredible Kingdom story shared throughout scripture. This love began to form in me as a sophomore in high school when I crossed the line of faith. Shortly after becoming a follower of Jesus, I received a Bible and was encouraged to read it regularly. I accepted the challenge and have remained committed to God's word for over five decades.

Along the way, however, I encountered seasons of dryness and boredom in my scripture reading. At times, I felt bound by a sense of legalistic obligation, measuring my success by my consistency or how much I read each day rather than by the depth of my engagement.

My breakthrough came when I discovered a more contemplative approach to engaging with the Bible. Ancient spiritual practices such as *Lectio Divina* and centering prayer became vital to my daily rhythm, helping to bring my mind and heart into greater balance. I was no longer just learning about God; I was experiencing him in a deeper, more personal way.

Over the years, I have woven breath prayers into my spiritual practice, drawing inspiration from simple yet profound phrases in scripture. I will never forget discovering this discipline during a two-week retreat with Dallas Willard as part of my doctoral program at Fuller Seminary. In one memorable conversation, Dallas introduced me to *The Jesus Prayer*, an ancient Eastern Orthodox practice dating back to the early centuries of Christianity. Monks would use the following phrase as a breath prayer, "Lord Jesus Christ, Son of God, have mercy on me, a sinner," and repeat it rhythmically to foster deep and continual communion with God.

Breath prayer is an ancient form of contemplative prayer that intertwines a simple portion of scripture or a phrase of truth with intentional, rhythmic breathing. This practice helps cultivate an awareness of God's presence, offering a way to remain anchored in him throughout the day. Because of its simplicity, breath prayer can be woven into the rhythm of daily life, providing a gentle yet powerful means to refocus one's heart and mind on the presence and promises of God.

At its core, breath prayer follows a natural pattern: The first portion of the prayer is meditated upon while inhaling slowly and the second portion while exhaling. This intentional practice is more than just a calming exercise; it is a spiritual discipline that invites deep communion with God.

Over the past two years, while reading through the Psalms, I decided to select a phrase from each Psalm to use as a breath prayer. I have been experimenting with this and have found it extremely beneficial. This book is one of the fruits of that experiment. As you engage with the breath prayers in this book, I trust you will experience their many benefits as I have firsthand.

The Difference Between Christian and Eastern Meditation Practices

Christian and Eastern meditation practices differ significantly in focus and purpose. Christian meditation emphasizes filling the mind with God's truth and presence through practices like those encouraged in this book. Its goal is not to empty the mind but to engage it deeply in communion with a personal God—seeking intimacy and alignment with him and his will. In contrast, Eastern meditation, common in traditions like Buddhism and Hinduism, often aims to empty the mind, detach from the self, and dissolve into an impersonal force or universal consciousness.

Because of these differences, some believers are wary of contemplative practices like meditation and centering prayer, concerned that they may drift too closely to Eastern methods and blur the line between biblical spirituality and non-Christian mysticism. Properly grounded Christian meditation, however, remains distinct in its purpose: Focus on a union with a loving, personal God through the guidance of his word and Spirit.

A Practice Both Ancient and Relevant

Breath prayer traces its roots to the Desert Fathers of the fourth and fifth centuries—spiritual seekers who withdrew into solitude to pursue deep communion with God. For generations, Christians have embraced this simple yet profound practice as a way to remain present with God amid the busyness of life.

Today, modern science echoes the wisdom of this ancient tradition. Therapists, mindfulness coaches, and even military trainers teach breathwork as a powerful tool to reduce stress, sharpen focus, and foster resilience. These insights affirm what believers have long understood: Our breath is a sacred gift—a bridge between body, mind, and spirit. Fittingly, in Hebrew and Greek, the biblical words for "breath" also mean "spirit," reminding us that every breath we take is infused with divine presence.

As you engage in the breath prayers found in *Breathing the Psalms*, you will likely experience many known benefits of focused breathing, such as reduced anxiety and increased mental clarity. Slow, deep breathing can help activate your vagus nerve, the most significant member of the central nervous system that impacts almost every vital organ in the human body. This kind of breathing releases toxic stress, thus calming one's mind and body and lowering one's blood pressure.[1]

Yet, my deeper prayer is that, beyond these physiological and emotional benefits, you will encounter God's transformational presence. As you pause to meditate on a brief passage from the Psalms, may the Spirit of God:

---

[1] Andrea Ganahl, *Victory Over Anxiety* (self-published, 2021), 116.
Wendy Hayden, *The Vagus Nerve Gut Brain Connection* (Self-published, 2023), chap. 6, "Breathing for Your Vagus Nerve."

- Calm and center you in his presence
- Speak to your heart and renew your mind
- Anchor you in your true identity as his beloved child, apart from your performance
- Revive you with his love, truth, and power from the inside out

And as you receive, may you also be led to pour out—to courageously share what you receive with others.

How to Use This Book

Breathing the Psalms is designed to help you slow down, settle into God's presence, and allow his word to shape and renew you. Each of the 150 exercises—one for each Psalm—follows a simple, repeatable pattern:

1. **Read the selected portion of the Psalm.**
   At the top of each exercise, you will find a passage from the Psalm. Read it slowly and thoughtfully multiple times.

2. **Pray the Psalm as a breath prayer.**
   Begin by taking a few slow, deep breaths, pausing briefly between each inhale and exhale. A helpful technique is to inhale slowly through your nose while thinking, "Smell the roses," and then exhale gently through your mouth while thinking, "Blow out the candles." Then, using the suggested breath prayer for focus, continue this practice for about three minutes. After some practice, you may want to experiment with adapting the suggested breath prayer to make it more personal and relevant or writing your own from scratch. Regularly engaging in this exercise can transform your mind, soul, and will.

3. **Listen in stillness.**
   Listening prayer is a simple but powerful way to create space to hear God's voice and experience his renewing presence. What does God's voice sound like? It is always loving and true, aligned with Jesus' words

and character. God speaks through thoughts and emotions in harmony with scripture.

4. **Journal what you sense God speaking.**
   After spending time in breath prayer and listening prayer, write down any key insights, thoughts, or impressions you received. What do you sense God is speaking to you?

5. **Write an "I will" statement in response.**
   Finally, ask God how you can respond in obedience to what you've learned. What action will you take? How will you put this into practice? With whom might you share what you learned or received?

To make the most of this practice, I encourage you to set aside some unhurried time in a quiet place, free from distractions (as much as is feasible—Grace to all you parents with young kids!). Experiment with what it looks like to "still your soul" before engaging with scripture. Take a moment to release any burdens to the Lord, inviting his Spirit to anoint your heart and mind.

Using a timer during this devotional practice can be incredibly helpful, and I encourage you to experiment with it as well. For instance, before beginning the breath prayer, try setting a timer for three to five minutes. This allows you to stay focused without being distracted by concerns about the passing time. Then, set another timer for the amount of time you'd like to spend in listening prayer and journaling. I typically choose 15 to 30 minutes for this part of the practice. Using a timer helps me resist the urge to prematurely step away from God's presence, giving me space to engage fully with his word and whispers. At the same time, it can also serve as a gentle boundary when I'm tempted to linger too long in reflection and journaling.

This book is meant to be interactive. So, with a pen in hand, be ready to record your reflections. More importantly, approach this journey with openness. Resist the urge to "get it right" or expect grand revelations every time. Spiritual formation is a process, and God meets us in both subtle and profound ways. If contemplative prayer is new for you, be patient with yourself and the journey. Simply give it a try and think of it as an experiment in encountering God in a fresh, life-giving way.

Many find that engaging in a practice like this with a friend or a small group can be especially encouraging. Consider inviting others to join you for a set time, sharing your experiences along the way.

To help you get started, I've created a free audio version of this breath prayer exercise, where I guide you through each segment. Use this QR code to access this resource.

Now, take a slow, deep breath… and let's begin.

PRAYING THE PSALMS
ONE BREATH AT A TIME

| Psalm 1:1-2 | *Blessed is the one who does not walk in step with the wicked or stand in the way that sinners take or sit in the company of mockers, but whose delight is in the law of the LORD, and who meditates on his law day and night.* |

Breath Prayer:

Begin with three slow, deep breaths. Pause briefly between each one. Then, for the next few minutes, prayerfully meditate on these phrases as you breathe:

- Inhale: *"I delight in your word, LORD."*
- Exhale: *"Help me meditate on it day and night."*

Listening Prayer:

I quiet my heart, turn my attention to Jesus, and simply listen. *What is God speaking to me through this Psalm and this time of meditation?*

Journal Reflection:

What did I sense during my breath or listening prayer? (Write freely here—thoughts, impressions, scriptures, images, or feelings.)

_____

_____

_____

_____

My "I Will" Statement:

How will I respond to this encounter with God's word? Whom can I share this with today?

_____

_____

Psalm 2:10-11

Therefore, you kings, be wise; be warned, you rulers of the earth. Serve the LORD with fear and celebrate his rule with trembling.

Breath Prayer:

Begin with three slow, deep breaths. Pause briefly between each one. Then, for the next few minutes, prayerfully meditate on these phrases as you breathe:

- Inhale: *"Help me remain in awe of you"*
- Exhale: *"as I serve you and celebrate your rule."*

Listening Prayer:

I quiet my heart, turn my attention to Jesus, and simply listen. *What is God speaking to me through this Psalm and this time of meditation?*

Journal Reflection:

What did I sense during my breath or listening prayer? (Write freely here—thoughts, impressions, scriptures, images, or feelings.)

_____

_____

_____

_____

My "I Will" Statement:

How will I respond to this encounter with God's word? Whom can I share this with today?

_____

_____

| Psalm 3:3-4 | *But you, LORD, are a shield around me, my glory, the One who lifts my head high. I call out to the LORD, and he answers me from his holy mountain.* |

Breath Prayer:

Begin with three slow, deep breaths. Pause briefly between each one. Then, for the next few minutes, prayerfully meditate on these phrases as you breathe:

- Inhale: *"Thank you, LORD, for being a shield around me"*
- Exhale: *"and the lifter of my head."*

Listening Prayer:

I quiet my heart, turn my attention to Jesus, and simply listen. *What is God speaking to me through this Psalm and this time of meditation?*

Journal Reflection:

What did I sense during my breath or listening prayer? (Write freely here—thoughts, impressions, scriptures, images, or feelings.)

_____
_____
_____
_____
_____

My "I Will" Statement:

How will I respond to this encounter with God's word? Whom can I share this with today?

_____
_____

| Psalm 4:6-8 | *Many, LORD, are asking, "Who will bring us prosperity?" Let the light of your face shine on us. Fill my heart with joy when their grain and new wine abound. In peace I will lie down and sleep, for you alone, LORD, make me dwell in safety.* |

Breath Prayer:

Begin with three slow, deep breaths. Pause briefly between each one. Then, for the next few minutes, prayerfully meditate on these phrases as you breathe:

- Inhale: *"Let your face shine upon me"*
- Exhale: *"and fill my heart with joy."*

Listening Prayer:

I quiet my heart, turn my attention to Jesus, and simply listen. *What is God speaking to me through this Psalm and this time of meditation?*

Journal Reflection:

What did I sense during my breath or listening prayer? (Write freely here—thoughts, impressions, scriptures, images, or feelings.)

_____

_____

_____

_____

_____

My "I Will" Statement:

How will I respond to this encounter with God's word? Whom can I share this with today?

_____

_____

> **Psalm 5:1-3**
>
> *Listen to my words, LORD, consider my lament. Hear my cry for help, my King and my God, for to you I pray. In the morning, LORD, you hear my voice; in the morning I lay my requests before you and wait expectantly.*

Breath Prayer:

Begin with three slow, deep breaths. Pause briefly between each one. Then, for the next few minutes, prayerfully meditate on these phrases as you breathe:

- Inhale: *"In the morning, you hear my voice"*
- Exhale: *"and I wait with expectation."*

Listening Prayer:

I quiet my heart, turn my attention to Jesus, and simply listen. *What is God speaking to me through this Psalm and this time of meditation?*

Journal Reflection:

What did I sense during my breath or listening prayer? (Write freely here—thoughts, impressions, scriptures, images, or feelings.)

_____

_____

_____

_____

_____

My "I Will" Statement:

How will I respond to this encounter with God's word? Whom can I share this with today?

_____

_____

> **Psalm 6:1-3**
>
> *LORD, do not rebuke me in your anger or discipline me in your wrath. Have mercy on me, LORD, for I am faint; heal me, LORD, for my bones are in agony. My soul is in deep anguish. How long, LORD, how long?*

Breath Prayer:

Begin with three slow, deep breaths. Pause briefly between each one. Then, for the next few minutes, prayerfully meditate on these phrases as you breathe:

- Inhale: *"Have mercy on me, LORD,"*
- Exhale: *"and heal me."*

Listening Prayer:

I quiet my heart, turn my attention to Jesus, and simply listen. *What is God speaking to me through this Psalm and this time of meditation?*

Journal Reflection:

What did I sense during my breath or listening prayer? (Write freely here—thoughts, impressions, scriptures, images, or feelings.)

_____

_____

_____

_____

My "I Will" Statement:

How will I respond to this encounter with God's word? Whom can I share this with today?

_____

_____

Psalm 7:10

My shield is God Most High, who saves the upright in heart.

Breath Prayer:

Begin with three slow, deep breaths. Pause briefly between each one. Then, for the next few minutes, prayerfully meditate on these phrases as you breathe:

- Inhale: *"You are my shield, God Most High,"*
- Exhale: *"the protector of the upright in heart."*

Listening Prayer:

I quiet my heart, turn my attention to Jesus, and simply listen. *What is God speaking to me through this Psalm and this time of meditation?*

Journal Reflection:

What did I sense during my breath or listening prayer? (Write freely here—thoughts, impressions, scriptures, images, or feelings.)

_____

_____

_____

_____

My "I Will" Statement:

How will I respond to this encounter with God's word? Whom can I share this with today?

_____

_____

| Psalm 8:1, 3-4 | *LORD, our Lord, how majestic is your name in all the earth!... When I consider your heavens, the work of your fingers, the moon and the stars, which you have set in place, what is mankind that you are mindful of them, human beings that you care for them.* |

Breath Prayer:

Begin with three slow, deep breaths. Pause briefly between each one. Then, for the next few minutes, prayerfully meditate on these phrases as you breathe:

- Inhale: *"How majestic is your name"*
- Exhale: *"in all the earth."*

Listening Prayer:

I quiet my heart, turn my attention to Jesus, and simply listen. *What is God speaking to me through this Psalm and this time of meditation?*

Journal Reflection:

What did I sense during my breath or listening prayer? (Write freely here—thoughts, impressions, scriptures, images, or feelings.)

_____

_____

_____

_____

_____

My "I Will" Statement:

How will I respond to this encounter with God's word? Whom can I share this with today?

_____

_____

| Psalm 9:1-2 | *I will give thanks to you, LORD, with all my heart; I will tell of all your wonderful deeds. I will be glad and rejoice in you; I will sing the praises of your name, O Most High.* |

Breath Prayer:

Begin with three slow, deep breaths. Pause briefly between each one. Then, for the next few minutes, prayerfully meditate on these phrases as you breathe:

- Inhale: *"I give thanks to you with all my heart;"*
- Exhale: *"I will be glad and rejoice in you."*

Listening Prayer:

I quiet my heart, turn my attention to Jesus, and simply listen. *What is God speaking to me through this Psalm and this time of meditation?*

Journal Reflection:

What did I sense during my breath or listening prayer? (Write freely here—thoughts, impressions, scriptures, images, or feelings.)

_____
_____
_____
_____

My "I Will" Statement:

How will I respond to this encounter with God's word? Whom can I share this with today?

_____
_____

| Psalm 10:16-18 | *The LORD is King for ever and ever; the nations will perish from his land. You, LORD, hear the desire of the afflicted; you encourage them, and you listen to their cry, defending the fatherless and the oppressed, so that mere earthly mortals will never again strike terror.* |

Breath Prayer:

Begin with three slow, deep breaths. Pause briefly between each one. Then, for the next few minutes, prayerfully meditate on these phrases as you breathe:

- Inhale: *"LORD, you who are King forever and ever,"*
- Exhale: *"hear the cry of the afflicted and encourage them."*

Listening Prayer:

I quiet my heart, turn my attention to Jesus, and simply listen. *What is God speaking to me through this Psalm and this time of meditation?*

Journal Reflection:

What did I sense during my breath or listening prayer? (Write freely here—thoughts, impressions, scriptures, images, or feelings.)

_____

_____

_____

_____

_____

My "I Will" Statement:

How will I respond to this encounter with God's word? Whom can I share this with today?

_____

_____

Psalm 11:7

*For the LORD is righteous, he loves justice;
the upright will see his face.*

Breath Prayer:

Begin with three slow, deep breaths. Pause briefly between each one. Then, for the next few minutes, prayerfully meditate on these phrases as you breathe:

- Inhale: *"You who are righteous and love justice,"*
- Exhale: *"I want to see your face!"*

Listening Prayer:

I quiet my heart, turn my attention to Jesus, and simply listen. *What is God speaking to me through this Psalm and this time of meditation?*

Journal Reflection:

What did I sense during my breath or listening prayer? (Write freely here—thoughts, impressions, scriptures, images, or feelings.)

_____

_____

_____

_____

My "I Will" Statement:

How will I respond to this encounter with God's word? Whom can I share this with today?

_____

_____

| Psalm 12:7-8 | *You, LORD, will keep the needy safe and will protect us forever from the wicked, who freely strut about when what is vile is honored by the human race.* |

Breath Prayer:

Begin with three slow, deep breaths. Pause briefly between each one. Then, for the next few minutes, prayerfully meditate on these phrases as you breathe:

- Inhale: *"LORD, you will keep me safe"*
- Exhale: *"and are always present to protect me."*

Listening Prayer:

I quiet my heart, turn my attention to Jesus, and simply listen. *What is God speaking to me through this Psalm and this time of meditation?*

Journal Reflection:

What did I sense during my breath or listening prayer? (Write freely here—thoughts, impressions, scriptures, images, or feelings.)

_____

_____

_____

_____

_____

My "I Will" Statement:

How will I respond to this encounter with God's word? Whom can I share this with today?

_____

_____

Psalm 13:5-6

But I trust in your unfailing love; my heart rejoices in your salvation. I will sing the LORD's praise, for he has been good to me.

Breath Prayer:

Begin with three slow, deep breaths. Pause briefly between each one. Then, for the next few minutes, prayerfully meditate on these phrases as you breathe:

- Inhale: *"I trust in your unfailing love"*
- Exhale: *"and rejoice in your salvation."*

Listening Prayer:

I quiet my heart, turn my attention to Jesus, and simply listen. *What is God speaking to me through this Psalm and this time of meditation?*

Journal Reflection:

What did I sense during my breath or listening prayer? (Write freely here—thoughts, impressions, scriptures, images, or feelings.)

_____
_____
_____
_____

My "I Will" Statement:

How will I respond to this encounter with God's word? Whom can I share this with today?

_____
_____

> **Psalm 14:4-6**
>
> *Do all these evildoers know nothing? They devour my people as though eating bread; they never call on the LORD. But there they are, overwhelmed with dread, for God is present in the company of the righteous. You evildoers frustrate the plans of the poor, but the LORD is their refuge.*

Breath Prayer:

Begin with three slow, deep breaths. Pause briefly between each one. Then, for the next few minutes, prayerfully meditate on these phrases as you breathe:

- Inhale: *"LORD, you are present with me,"*
- Exhale: *"and you are my refuge."*

Listening Prayer:

I quiet my heart, turn my attention to Jesus, and simply listen. *What is God speaking to me through this Psalm and this time of meditation?*

Journal Reflection:

What did I sense during my breath or listening prayer? (Write freely here—thoughts, impressions, scriptures, images, or feelings.)

_____

_____

_____

_____

_____

My "I Will" Statement:

How will I respond to this encounter with God's word? Whom can I share this with today?

_____

_____

| Psalm 15:1-3, 5 | *LORD, who may dwell in your sacred tent? Who may live on your holy mountain? The one whose walk is blameless, who does what is righteous, who speaks the truth from their heart; whose tongue utters no slander, who does no wrong to a neighbor, and casts no slur on others.... Whoever does these things will never be shaken.* |

Breath Prayer:

Begin with three slow, deep breaths. Pause briefly between each one. Then, for the next few minutes, prayerfully meditate on these phrases as you breathe:

- Inhale: *"LORD, I yearn to dwell with you"*
- Exhale: *"and never be shaken."*

Listening Prayer:

I quiet my heart, turn my attention to Jesus, and simply listen. *What is God speaking to me through this Psalm and this time of meditation?*

Journal Reflection:

What did I sense during my breath or listening prayer? (Write freely here—thoughts, impressions, scriptures, images, or feelings.)

_____

_____

_____

_____

My "I Will" Statement:

How will I respond to this encounter with God's word? Whom can I share this with today?

_____

_____

| **Psalm 16:8-9** | *I keep my eyes always on the LORD. With him at my right hand, I will not be shaken. Therefore my heart is glad and my tongue rejoices; my body also will rest secure.* |

Breath Prayer:

Begin with three slow, deep breaths. Pause briefly between each one. Then, for the next few minutes, prayerfully meditate on these phrases as you breathe:

- Inhale: *"Help me keep my eyes"*
- Exhale: *"always on you, LORD."*

Listening Prayer:

I quiet my heart, turn my attention to Jesus, and simply listen. *What is God speaking to me through this Psalm and this time of meditation?*

Journal Reflection:

What did I sense during my breath or listening prayer? (Write freely here—thoughts, impressions, scriptures, images, or feelings.)

_____

_____

_____

_____

_____

My "I Will" Statement:

How will I respond to this encounter with God's word? Whom can I share this with today?

_____

_____

Psalm 17:7-8	*Show me the wonders of your great love.... Keep me as the apple of your eye; hide me in the shadow of your wings.*

Breath Prayer:

Begin with three slow, deep breaths. Pause briefly between each one. Then, for the next few minutes, prayerfully meditate on these phrases as you breathe:

- Inhale: *"Keep me as the apple of your eye"*
- Exhale: *"and hide me in the shadow of your wings."*

Listening Prayer:

I quiet my heart, turn my attention to Jesus, and simply listen. *What is God speaking to me through this Psalm and this time of meditation?*

Journal Reflection:

What did I sense during my breath or listening prayer? (Write freely here—thoughts, impressions, scriptures, images, or feelings.)

_____
_____
_____
_____

My "I Will" Statement:

How will I respond to this encounter with God's word? Whom can I share this with today?

_____
_____

Psalm 18:28-29

You, LORD, keep my lamp burning; my God turns my darkness into light. With your help I can advance against a troop; with my God I can scale a wall.

Breath Prayer:

Begin with three slow, deep breaths. Pause briefly between each one. Then, for the next few minutes, prayerfully meditate on these phrases as you breathe:

- Inhale: *"You keep my lamp burning"*
- Exhale: *"and turn my darkness into light."*

Listening Prayer:

I quiet my heart, turn my attention to Jesus, and simply listen. *What is God speaking to me through this Psalm and this time of meditation?*

Journal Reflection:

What did I sense during my breath or listening prayer? (Write freely here—thoughts, impressions, scriptures, images, or feelings.)

_____

_____

_____

_____

My "I Will" Statement:

How will I respond to this encounter with God's word? Whom can I share this with today?

_____

_____

| Psalm 19:7-8 | *The law of the Lord is perfect, refreshing the soul. The statutes of the LORD are trustworthy, making wise the simple. The precepts of the LORD are right, giving joy to the heart. The commands of the LORD are radiant, giving light to the eyes.* |

Breath Prayer:

Begin with three slow, deep breaths. Pause briefly between each one. Then, for the next few minutes, prayerfully meditate on these phrases as you breathe:

- Inhale: *"Your word refreshes my soul"*
- Exhale: *"and brings joy to my heart and light to my eyes."*

Listening Prayer:

I quiet my heart, turn my attention to Jesus, and simply listen. *What is God speaking to me through this Psalm and this time of meditation?*

Journal Reflection:

What did I sense during my breath or listening prayer? (Write freely here—thoughts, impressions, scriptures, images, or feelings.)

_____
_____
_____
_____
_____

My "I Will" Statement:

How will I respond to this encounter with God's word? Whom can I share this with today?

_____
_____

Psalm 20:7

Some trust in chariots and some in horses, but we trust in the name of the LORD our God.

Breath Prayer:

Begin with three slow, deep breaths. Pause briefly between each one. Then, for the next few minutes, prayerfully meditate on these phrases as you breathe:

- Inhale: *"I put my trust in you, LORD,"*
- Exhale: *"not in anyone or anything else."*

Listening Prayer:

I quiet my heart, turn my attention to Jesus, and simply listen. *What is God speaking to me through this Psalm and this time of meditation?*

Journal Reflection:

What did I sense during my breath or listening prayer? (Write freely here—thoughts, impressions, scriptures, images, or feelings.)

_____

_____

_____

_____

_____

My "I Will" Statement:

How will I respond to this encounter with God's word? Whom can I share this with today?

_____

_____

> **Psalm 21:7** — *For the king trusts in the LORD; through the unfailing love of the Most High he will not be shaken.*

Breath Prayer:

Begin with three slow, deep breaths. Pause briefly between each one. Then, for the next few minutes, prayerfully meditate on these phrases as you breathe:

- Inhale: *"Through your unfailing love,"*
- Exhale: *"I will not be shaken."*

Listening Prayer:

I quiet my heart, turn my attention to Jesus, and simply listen. *What is God speaking to me through this Psalm and this time of meditation?*

Journal Reflection:

What did I sense during my breath or listening prayer? (Write freely here—thoughts, impressions, scriptures, images, or feelings.)

_____
_____
_____
_____
_____

My "I Will" Statement:

How will I respond to this encounter with God's word? Whom can I share this with today?

_____
_____

| Psalm 22:19 | *But you, LORD, do not be far from me. You are my strength; come quickly to help me.* |

Breath Prayer:

Begin with three slow, deep breaths. Pause briefly between each one. Then, for the next few minutes, prayerfully meditate on these phrases as you breathe:

- Inhale: *"You are my strength;"*
- Exhale: *"come quickly to help me."*

Listening Prayer:

I quiet my heart, turn my attention to Jesus, and simply listen. *What is God speaking to me through this Psalm and this time of meditation?*

Journal Reflection:

What did I sense during my breath or listening prayer? (Write freely here—thoughts, impressions, scriptures, images, or feelings.)

_____

_____

_____

_____

My "I Will" Statement:

How will I respond to this encounter with God's word? Whom can I share this with today?

_____

_____

| Psalm 23:1, 4 | The LORD is my shepherd, I lack nothing.... Even though I walk through the darkest valley, I will fear no evil, for you are with me; your rod and your staff, they comfort me. |

Breath Prayer:

Begin with three slow, deep breaths. Pause briefly between each one. Then, for the next few minutes, prayerfully meditate on these phrases as you breathe:

- Inhale: *"I will fear no evil,"*
- Exhale: *"for you are with me."*

Listening Prayer:

I quiet my heart, turn my attention to Jesus, and simply listen. *What is God speaking to me through this Psalm and this time of meditation?*

Journal Reflection:

What did I sense during my breath or listening prayer? (Write freely here—thoughts, impressions, scriptures, images, or feelings.)

_____

_____

_____

_____

My "I Will" Statement:

How will I respond to this encounter with God's word? Whom can I share this with today?

_____

_____

Psalm 24:7-8

Lift up your heads, you gates; be lifted up, you ancient doors, that the King of glory may come in. Who is this King of glory? The LORD strong and mighty, the LORD mighty in battle.

Breath Prayer:

Begin with three slow, deep breaths. Pause briefly between each one. Then, for the next few minutes, prayerfully meditate on these phrases as you breathe:

- Inhale: *"Be lifted up, you ancient doors,"*
- Exhale: *"that the King of glory may come in."*

Listening Prayer:

I quiet my heart, turn my attention to Jesus, and simply listen. *What is God speaking to me through this Psalm and this time of meditation?*

Journal Reflection:

What did I sense during my breath or listening prayer? (Write freely here—thoughts, impressions, scriptures, images, or feelings.)

_____

_____

_____

_____

_____

My "I Will" Statement:

How will I respond to this encounter with God's word? Whom can I share this with today?

_____

_____

Psalm 25:4-5

Show me your ways, LORD, teach me your paths. Guide me in your truth and teach me, for you are God my Savior, and my hope is in you all day long.

Breath Prayer:

Begin with three slow, deep breaths. Pause briefly between each one. Then, for the next few minutes, prayerfully meditate on these phrases as you breathe:

- Inhale: *"Help me put my hope in you"*
- Exhale: *"all day long."*

Listening Prayer:

I quiet my heart, turn my attention to Jesus, and simply listen. *What is God speaking to me through this Psalm and this time of meditation?*

Journal Reflection:

What did I sense during my breath or listening prayer? (Write freely here—thoughts, impressions, scriptures, images, or feelings.)

_____

_____

_____

_____

_____

My "I Will" Statement:

How will I respond to this encounter with God's word? Whom can I share this with today?

_____

_____

Psalm 26:2-3

Test me, LORD, and try me, examine my heart and my mind; for I have always been mindful of your unfailing love and have lived in reliance on your faithfulness.

Breath Prayer:

Begin with three slow, deep breaths. Pause briefly between each one. Then, for the next few minutes, prayerfully meditate on these phrases as you breathe:

- Inhale: *"Help me remain mindful of your unfailing love"*
- Exhale: *"and rely on your faithfulness."*

Listening Prayer:

I quiet my heart, turn my attention to Jesus, and simply listen. *What is God speaking to me through this Psalm and this time of meditation?*

Journal Reflection:

What did I sense during my breath or listening prayer? (Write freely here—thoughts, impressions, scriptures, images, or feelings.)

_____

_____

_____

_____

My "I Will" Statement:

How will I respond to this encounter with God's word? Whom can I share this with today?

_____

_____

| Psalm 27:4, 8 | *One thing I ask from the LORD, this only do I seek: that I may dwell in the house of the LORD all the days of my life, to gaze on the beauty of the Lord and to seek him in his temple.... My heart says of you, "Seek his face!" Your face, LORD, I will seek.* |

Breath Prayer:

Begin with three slow, deep breaths. Pause briefly between each one. Then, for the next few minutes, prayerfully meditate on these phrases as you breathe:

- Inhale: *"My heart says of you, 'Seek his face!'"*
- Exhale: *"Your face, LORD, I will seek."*

Listening Prayer:

I quiet my heart, turn my attention to Jesus, and simply listen. *What is God speaking to me through this Psalm and this time of meditation?*

Journal Reflection:

What did I sense during my breath or listening prayer? (Write freely here—thoughts, impressions, scriptures, images, or feelings.)

_____
_____
_____
_____
_____

My "I Will" Statement:

How will I respond to this encounter with God's word? Whom can I share this with today?

_____
_____

| Psalm 28:6-7 | *Praise be to the LORD, for he has heard my cry for mercy. The LORD is my strength and my shield; my heart trusts in him, and he helps me. My heart leaps for joy, and with my song I praise him.* |

Breath Prayer:

Begin with three slow, deep breaths. Pause briefly between each one. Then, for the next few minutes, prayerfully meditate on these phrases as you breathe:

- Inhale: *"Thank you for hearing my prayer"*
- Exhale: *"and filling my heart with joy and praise."*

Listening Prayer:

I quiet my heart, turn my attention to Jesus, and simply listen. *What is God speaking to me through this Psalm and this time of meditation?*

Journal Reflection:

What did I sense during my breath or listening prayer? (Write freely here—thoughts, impressions, scriptures, images, or feelings.)

_____

_____

_____

_____

_____

My "I Will" Statement:

How will I respond to this encounter with God's word? Whom can I share this with today?

_____

_____

> **Psalm 29:4, 11**
>
> *The voice of the LORD is powerful; the voice of the LORD is majestic. The Lord gives strength to his people; the LORD blesses his people with peace.*

Breath Prayer:

Begin with three slow, deep breaths. Pause briefly between each one. Then, for the next few minutes, prayerfully meditate on these phrases as you breathe:

- Inhale: *"Help me hear your powerful and majestic voice"*
- Exhale: *"that blesses me with strength and peace."*

Listening Prayer:

I quiet my heart, turn my attention to Jesus, and simply listen. *What is God speaking to me through this Psalm and this time of meditation?*

Journal Reflection:

What did I sense during my breath or listening prayer? (Write freely here—thoughts, impressions, scriptures, images, or feelings.)

_____

_____

_____

_____

_____

My "I Will" Statement:

How will I respond to this encounter with God's word? Whom can I share this with today?

_____

_____

Psalm 30:11-12

You turned my wailing into dancing; you removed my sackcloth and clothed me with joy, that my heart may sing your praises and not be silent.

Breath Prayer:

Begin with three slow, deep breaths. Pause briefly between each one. Then, for the next few minutes, prayerfully meditate on these phrases as you breathe:

- Inhale: *"LORD, please turn my sadness into celebration"*
- Exhale: *"and fill me with your joy."*

Listening Prayer:

I quiet my heart, turn my attention to Jesus, and simply listen. *What is God speaking to me through this Psalm and this time of meditation?*

Journal Reflection:

What did I sense during my breath or listening prayer? (Write freely here—thoughts, impressions, scriptures, images, or feelings.)

_____
_____
_____
_____
_____

My "I Will" Statement:

How will I respond to this encounter with God's word? Whom can I share this with today?

_____
_____

| Psalm 31:3-4 | *Since you are my rock and my fortress, for the sake of your name lead and guide me. Keep me free from the trap that is set for me, for you are my refuge.* |

Breath Prayer:

Begin with three slow, deep breaths. Pause briefly between each one. Then, for the next few minutes, prayerfully meditate on these phrases as you breathe:

- Inhale: *"Lead and guide me today"*
- Exhale: *"and keep me free from the trap of the enemy."*

Listening Prayer:

I quiet my heart, turn my attention to Jesus, and simply listen. *What is God speaking to me through this Psalm and this time of meditation?*

Journal Reflection:

What did I sense during my breath or listening prayer? (Write freely here—thoughts, impressions, scriptures, images, or feelings.)

_____

_____

_____

_____

_____

My "I Will" Statement:

How will I respond to this encounter with God's word? Whom can I share this with today?

_____

_____

Psalm 32:8

I will instruct you and teach you in the way you should go; I will counsel you with my loving eye on you.

Breath Prayer:

Begin with three slow, deep breaths. Pause briefly between each one. Then, for the next few minutes, prayerfully meditate on these phrases as you breathe:

- Inhale: *"Thank you for counseling me"*
- Exhale: *"with your loving eye upon me."*

Listening Prayer:

I quiet my heart, turn my attention to Jesus, and simply listen. *What is God speaking to me through this Psalm and this time of meditation?*

Journal Reflection:

What did I sense during my breath or listening prayer? (Write freely here—thoughts, impressions, scriptures, images, or feelings.)

_____

_____

_____

_____

_____

My "I Will" Statement:

How will I respond to this encounter with God's word? Whom can I share this with today?

_____

_____

Psalm 33:10-11

The LORD foils the plans of the nations; he thwarts the purposes of the peoples. But the plans of the LORD stand firm forever, the purposes of his heart through all generations.

Breath Prayer:

Begin with three slow, deep breaths. Pause briefly between each one. Then, for the next few minutes, prayerfully meditate on these phrases as you breathe:

- Inhale: *"Reveal to me your plans and purposes,"*
- Exhale: *"which stand firm through all generations."*

Listening Prayer:

I quiet my heart, turn my attention to Jesus, and simply listen. *What is God speaking to me through this Psalm and this time of meditation?*

Journal Reflection:

What did I sense during my breath or listening prayer? (Write freely here—thoughts, impressions, scriptures, images, or feelings.)

_____

_____

_____

_____

My "I Will" Statement:

How will I respond to this encounter with God's word? Whom can I share this with today?

_____

_____

> **Psalm 34:8-9**
>
> *Taste and see that the LORD is good; blessed is the one who takes refuge in him. Fear the LORD, you his holy people, for those who fear him lack nothing.*

Breath Prayer:

Begin with three slow, deep breaths. Pause briefly between each one. Then, for the next few minutes, prayerfully meditate on these phrases as you breathe:

- Inhale: *"I will taste and see that you are good"*
- Exhale: *"and take refuge in you."*

Listening Prayer:

I quiet my heart, turn my attention to Jesus, and simply listen. *What is God speaking to me through this Psalm and this time of meditation?*

Journal Reflection:

What did I sense during my breath or listening prayer? (Write freely here—thoughts, impressions, scriptures, images, or feelings.)

_____

_____

_____

_____

_____

My "I Will" Statement:

How will I respond to this encounter with God's word? Whom can I share this with today?

_____

_____

Psalm 35:1-2

Contend, LORD, with those who contend with me; fight against those who fight against me. Take up shield and armor; arise and come to my aid.

Breath Prayer:

Begin with three slow, deep breaths. Pause briefly between each one. Then, for the next few minutes, prayerfully meditate on these phrases as you breathe:

- Inhale: *"Fight against those who fight against me;"*
- Exhale: *"arise and come to my aid."*

Listening Prayer:

I quiet my heart, turn my attention to Jesus, and simply listen. *What is God speaking to me through this Psalm and this time of meditation?*

Journal Reflection:

What did I sense during my breath or listening prayer? (Write freely here—thoughts, impressions, scriptures, images, or feelings.)

_____

_____

_____

_____

_____

My "I Will" Statement:

How will I respond to this encounter with God's word? Whom can I share this with today?

_____

_____

> **Psalm 36:7-9**
>
> *How priceless is your unfailing love, O God! People take refuge in the shadow of your wings. They feast on the abundance of your house; you give them drink from your river of delights. For with you is the fountain of life; in your light we see light.*

Breath Prayer:

Begin with three slow, deep breaths. Pause briefly between each one. Then, for the next few minutes, prayerfully meditate on these phrases as you breathe:

- Inhale: *"You are my fountain of life,"*
- Exhale: *"and in your light, I see light."*

Listening Prayer:

I quiet my heart, turn my attention to Jesus, and simply listen. *What is God speaking to me through this Psalm and this time of meditation?*

Journal Reflection:

What did I sense during my breath or listening prayer? (Write freely here—thoughts, impressions, scriptures, images, or feelings.)

_____
_____
_____
_____
_____

My "I Will" Statement:

How will I respond to this encounter with God's word? Whom can I share this with today?

_____
_____

| Psalm 37:3-4 | *Trust in the LORD and do good; dwell in the land and enjoy safe pasture. Take delight in the LORD, and he will give you the desires of your heart.* |

Breath Prayer:

Begin with three slow, deep breaths. Pause briefly between each one. Then, for the next few minutes, prayerfully meditate on these phrases as you breathe:

- Inhale: *"I delight in you, LORD,"*
- Exhale: *"and from you receive the desires of my heart."*

Listening Prayer:

I quiet my heart, turn my attention to Jesus, and simply listen. *What is God speaking to me through this Psalm and this time of meditation?*

Journal Reflection:

What did I sense during my breath or listening prayer? (Write freely here—thoughts, impressions, scriptures, images, or feelings.)

_____

_____

_____

_____

_____

My "I Will" Statement:

How will I respond to this encounter with God's word? Whom can I share this with today?

_____

_____

Psalm 38:15

LORD, I wait for you; you will answer, Lord my God.

Breath Prayer:

Begin with three slow, deep breaths. Pause briefly between each one. Then, for the next few minutes, prayerfully meditate on these phrases as you breathe:

- Inhale: *"LORD, I will wait"*
- Exhale: *"for you to answer."*

Listening Prayer:

I quiet my heart, turn my attention to Jesus, and simply listen. *What is God speaking to me through this Psalm and this time of meditation?*

Journal Reflection:

What did I sense during my breath or listening prayer? (Write freely here—thoughts, impressions, scriptures, images, or feelings.)

_____

_____

_____

_____

My "I Will" Statement:

How will I respond to this encounter with God's word? Whom can I share this with today?

_____

_____

| Psalm 39:7 | *Surely everyone goes around like a mere phantom; in vain they rush about, heaping up wealth without knowing whose it will finally be. But now, Lord, what do I look for? My hope is in you.* |

Breath Prayer:

Begin with three slow, deep breaths. Pause briefly between each one. Then, for the next few minutes, prayerfully meditate on these phrases as you breathe:

- Inhale: *"Lord, you know what I look for;"*
- Exhale: *"my hope is in you."*

Listening Prayer:

I quiet my heart, turn my attention to Jesus, and simply listen. *What is God speaking to me through this Psalm and this time of meditation?*

Journal Reflection:

What did I sense during my breath or listening prayer? (Write freely here—thoughts, impressions, scriptures, images, or feelings.)

_____

_____

_____

_____

_____

My "I Will" Statement:

How will I respond to this encounter with God's word? Whom can I share this with today?

_____

_____

Psalm 40:7-8

Then I said, "Here I am, I have come—it is written about me in the scroll. I desire to do your will, my God; your law is within my heart."

Breath Prayer:

Begin with three slow, deep breaths. Pause briefly between each one. Then, for the next few minutes, prayerfully meditate on these phrases as you breathe:

- Inhale: *"Here I am, God;"*
- Exhale: *"I desire to do your will."*

Listening Prayer:

I quiet my heart, turn my attention to Jesus, and simply listen. *What is God speaking to me through this Psalm and this time of meditation?*

Journal Reflection:

What did I sense during my breath or listening prayer? (Write freely here—thoughts, impressions, scriptures, images, or feelings.)

_____

_____

_____

_____

_____

My "I Will" Statement:

How will I respond to this encounter with God's word? Whom can I share this with today?

_____

_____

Psalm 41:12-13

Because of my integrity you uphold me and set me in your presence forever. Praise be to the LORD, the God of Israel, from everlasting to everlasting. Amen and Amen.

Breath Prayer:

Begin with three slow, deep breaths. Pause briefly between each one. Then, for the next few minutes, prayerfully meditate on these phrases as you breathe:

- Inhale: *"Thank you for upholding me"*
- Exhale: *"and always being with me."*

Listening Prayer:

I quiet my heart, turn my attention to Jesus, and simply listen. *What is God speaking to me through this Psalm and this time of meditation?*

Journal Reflection:

What did I sense during my breath or listening prayer? (Write freely here—thoughts, impressions, scriptures, images, or feelings.)

_____

_____

_____

_____

My "I Will" Statement:

How will I respond to this encounter with God's word? Whom can I share this with today?

_____

_____

| Psalm 42:1-2 | *As the deer pants for streams of water, so my soul pants for you, my God. My soul thirsts for God, for the living God. When can I go and meet with God?* |

Breath Prayer:

Begin with three slow, deep breaths. Pause briefly between each one. Then, for the next few minutes, prayerfully meditate on these phrases as you breathe:

- Inhale: *"As the deer pants for streams of water,"*
- Exhale: *"so my soul pants for you, my God."*

Listening Prayer:

I quiet my heart, turn my attention to Jesus, and simply listen. *What is God speaking to me through this Psalm and this time of meditation?*

Journal Reflection:

What did I sense during my breath or listening prayer? (Write freely here—thoughts, impressions, scriptures, images, or feelings.)

_____
_____
_____
_____
_____

My "I Will" Statement:

How will I respond to this encounter with God's word? Whom can I share this with today?

_____
_____

> **Psalm 43:5**
>
> *Why, my soul, are you downcast? Why so disturbed within me? Put your hope in God, for I will yet praise him, my Savior and my God.*

Breath Prayer:

Begin with three slow, deep breaths. Pause briefly between each one. Then, for the next few minutes, prayerfully meditate on these phrases as you breathe:

- Inhale: *"When my soul is downcast or disturbed,"*
- Exhale: *"help me put my hope in you, my Savior."*

Listening Prayer:

I quiet my heart, turn my attention to Jesus, and simply listen. *What is God speaking to me through this Psalm and this time of meditation?*

Journal Reflection:

What did I sense during my breath or listening prayer? (Write freely here—thoughts, impressions, scriptures, images, or feelings.)

_____
_____
_____
_____
_____

My "I Will" Statement:

How will I respond to this encounter with God's word? Whom can I share this with today?

_____
_____

> **Psalm 44:3**
> *It was not by their sword that they won the land, nor did their arm bring them victory; it was your right hand, your arm, and the light of your face, for you loved them.*

Breath Prayer:

Begin with three slow, deep breaths. Pause briefly between each one. Then, for the next few minutes, prayerfully meditate on these phrases as you breathe:

- Inhale: *"Your right hand and the light of your face"*
- Exhale: *"bring victory to your beloved."*

Listening Prayer:

I quiet my heart, turn my attention to Jesus, and simply listen. *What is God speaking to me through this Psalm and this time of meditation?*

Journal Reflection:

What did I sense during my breath or listening prayer? (Write freely here—thoughts, impressions, scriptures, images, or feelings.)

_____

_____

_____

_____

_____

My "I Will" Statement:

How will I respond to this encounter with God's word? Whom can I share this with today?

_____

_____

Psalm 45:1

My heart is stirred by a noble theme as I recite my verses for the king; my tongue is the pen of a skillful writer.

Breath Prayer:

Begin with three slow, deep breaths. Pause briefly between each one. Then, for the next few minutes, prayerfully meditate on these phrases as you breathe:

- Inhale: *"Thank you, Lord, for stirring my heart"*
- Exhale: *"as I ponder your word in your presence."*

Listening Prayer:

I quiet my heart, turn my attention to Jesus, and simply listen. *What is God speaking to me through this Psalm and this time of meditation?*

Journal Reflection:

What did I sense during my breath or listening prayer? (Write freely here—thoughts, impressions, scriptures, images, or feelings.)

_____

_____

_____

_____

_____

My "I Will" Statement:

How will I respond to this encounter with God's word? Whom can I share this with today?

_____

_____

> **Psalm 46:10**
>
> *He says, "Be still, and know that I am God; I will be exalted among the nations, I will be exalted in the earth."*

Breath Prayer:

Begin with three slow, deep breaths. Pause briefly between each one. Then, for the next few minutes, prayerfully meditate on these phrases as you breathe:

- Inhale: *"Lord, help me be still"*
- Exhale: *"and experientially know that you are God."*

Listening Prayer:

I quiet my heart, turn my attention to Jesus, and simply listen. *What is God speaking to me through this Psalm and this time of meditation?*

Journal Reflection:

What did I sense during my breath or listening prayer? (Write freely here—thoughts, impressions, scriptures, images, or feelings.)

_____

_____

_____

_____

_____

My "I Will" Statement:

How will I respond to this encounter with God's word? Whom can I share this with today?

_____

_____

Psalm 47:1-2	*Clap your hands, all you nations; shout to God with cries of joy. For the LORD Most High is awesome, the great King over all the earth.*

Breath Prayer:

Begin with three slow, deep breaths. Pause briefly between each one. Then, for the next few minutes, prayerfully meditate on these phrases as you breathe:

- Inhale: *"LORD Most High, you are awesome,"*
- Exhale: *"the great King over all the earth."*

Listening Prayer:

I quiet my heart, turn my attention to Jesus, and simply listen. *What is God speaking to me through this Psalm and this time of meditation?*

Journal Reflection:

What did I sense during my breath or listening prayer? (Write freely here—thoughts, impressions, scriptures, images, or feelings.)

_____

_____

_____

_____

_____

My "I Will" Statement:

How will I respond to this encounter with God's word? Whom can I share this with today?

_____

_____

Psalm 48:9-10	*Within your temple, O God, we meditate on your unfailing love. Like your name, O God, your praise reaches to the ends of the earth; your right hand is filled with righteousness.*

Breath Prayer:

Begin with three slow, deep breaths. Pause briefly between each one. Then, for the next few minutes, prayerfully meditate on these phrases as you breathe:

- Inhale: *"In your presence, O God,"*
- Exhale: *"I meditate on your unfailing love."*

Listening Prayer:

I quiet my heart, turn my attention to Jesus, and simply listen. *What is God speaking to me through this Psalm and this time of meditation?*

Journal Reflection:

What did I sense during my breath or listening prayer? (Write freely here—thoughts, impressions, scriptures, images, or feelings.)

_____

_____

_____

_____

My "I Will" Statement:

How will I respond to this encounter with God's word? Whom can I share this with today?

_____

_____

Psalm 49:15-17	*But God will redeem me from the realm of the dead; he will surely take me to himself. Do not be overawed when others grow rich, when the splendor of their houses increases; for they will take nothing with them when they die, their splendor will not descend with them.*

Breath Prayer:

Begin with three slow, deep breaths. Pause briefly between each one. Then, for the next few minutes, prayerfully meditate on these phrases as you breathe:

- Inhale: *"Protect me from the lust of wealth,"*
- Exhale: *"for no one can take riches with them when they die."*

Listening Prayer:

I quiet my heart, turn my attention to Jesus, and simply listen. *What is God speaking to me through this Psalm and this time of meditation?*

Journal Reflection:

What did I sense during my breath or listening prayer? (Write freely here—thoughts, impressions, scriptures, images, or feelings.)

_____
_____
_____
_____
_____

My "I Will" Statement:

How will I respond to this encounter with God's word? Whom can I share this with today?

_____
_____

| **Psalm 50:3** | *Our God comes and will not be silent; a fire devours before him, and around him a tempest rages.* |

Breath Prayer:

Begin with three slow, deep breaths. Pause briefly between each one. Then, for the next few minutes, prayerfully meditate on these phrases as you breathe:

- Inhale: *"God, join me now in prayer,"*
- Exhale: *"and please do not be silent."*

Listening Prayer:

I quiet my heart, turn my attention to Jesus, and simply listen. *What is God speaking to me through this Psalm and this time of meditation?*

Journal Reflection:

What did I sense during my breath or listening prayer? (Write freely here—thoughts, impressions, scriptures, images, or feelings.)

_____
_____
_____
_____
_____

My "I Will" Statement:

How will I respond to this encounter with God's word? Whom can I share this with today?

_____
_____

> **Psalm 51:10-12**
> *Create in me a pure heart, O God, and renew a steadfast spirit within me. Do not cast me from your presence or take your Holy Spirit from me. Restore to me the joy of your salvation and grant me a willing spirit, to sustain me.*

Breath Prayer:

Begin with three slow, deep breaths. Pause briefly between each one. Then, for the next few minutes, prayerfully meditate on these phrases as you breathe:

- Inhale: *"Create in me a clean heart, O God,"*
- Exhale: *"and renew a steadfast spirit within me."*

Listening Prayer:

I quiet my heart, turn my attention to Jesus, and simply listen. *What is God speaking to me through this Psalm and this time of meditation?*

Journal Reflection:

What did I sense during my breath or listening prayer? (Write freely here—thoughts, impressions, scriptures, images, or feelings.)

_____

_____

_____

_____

_____

My "I Will" Statement:

How will I respond to this encounter with God's word? Whom can I share this with today?

_____

_____

> **Psalm 52:9**
>
> *For what you have done I will always praise you in the presence of your faithful people. And I will hope in your name, for your name is good.*

Breath Prayer:

Begin with three slow, deep breaths. Pause briefly between each one. Then, for the next few minutes, prayerfully meditate on these phrases as you breathe:

- Inhale: *"I praise you for what you have done,"*
- Exhale: *"and put my hope in your name."*

Listening Prayer:

I quiet my heart, turn my attention to Jesus, and simply listen. *What is God speaking to me through this Psalm and this time of meditation?*

Journal Reflection:

What did I sense during my breath or listening prayer? (Write freely here—thoughts, impressions, scriptures, images, or feelings.)

_____

_____

_____

_____

My "I Will" Statement:

How will I respond to this encounter with God's word? Whom can I share this with today?

_____

_____

Psalm 53:6

Oh, that salvation for Israel would come out of Zion! When God restores his people, let Jacob rejoice and Israel be glad!

Breath Prayer:

Begin with three slow, deep breaths. Pause briefly between each one. Then, for the next few minutes, prayerfully meditate on these phrases as you breathe:

- Inhale: *"God, you will restore your people,"*
- Exhale: *"so I will rejoice and be glad!"*

Listening Prayer:

I quiet my heart, turn my attention to Jesus, and simply listen. *What is God speaking to me through this Psalm and this time of meditation?*

Journal Reflection:

What did I sense during my breath or listening prayer? (Write freely here—thoughts, impressions, scriptures, images, or feelings.)

_____

_____

_____

_____

My "I Will" Statement:

How will I respond to this encounter with God's word? Whom can I share this with today?

_____

_____

| Psalm 54:1-4 | *Save me, O God, by your name; vindicate me by your might. Hear my prayer, O God; listen to the words of my mouth. Arrogant foes are attacking me; ruthless people are trying to kill me—people without regard for God. Surely God is my help; the Lord is the one who sustains me.* |

Breath Prayer:

Begin with three slow, deep breaths. Pause briefly between each one. Then, for the next few minutes, prayerfully meditate on these phrases as you breathe:

- Inhale: *"Hear my prayer, O God,"*
- Exhale: *"for you are my help and the one who sustains me."*

Listening Prayer:

I quiet my heart, turn my attention to Jesus, and simply listen. *What is God speaking to me through this Psalm and this time of meditation?*

Journal Reflection:

What did I sense during my breath or listening prayer? (Write freely here—thoughts, impressions, scriptures, images, or feelings.)

_____
_____
_____
_____
_____

My "I Will" Statement:

How will I respond to this encounter with God's word? Whom can I share this with today?

_____
_____

Psalm 55:22

*Cast your cares on the LORD and he will sustain you;
he will never let the righteous be shaken.*

Breath Prayer:

Begin with three slow, deep breaths. Pause briefly between each one. Then, for the next few minutes, prayerfully meditate on these phrases as you breathe:

- Inhale: *"I cast my cares on you, LORD,"*
- Exhale: *"and trust that you will sustain me."*

Listening Prayer:

I quiet my heart, turn my attention to Jesus, and simply listen. *What is God speaking to me through this Psalm and this time of meditation?*

Journal Reflection:

What did I sense during my breath or listening prayer? (Write freely here—thoughts, impressions, scriptures, images, or feelings.)

_____

_____

_____

_____

_____

My "I Will" Statement:

How will I respond to this encounter with God's word? Whom can I share this with today?

_____

_____

Psalm 56:3-4

When I am afraid, I put my trust in you. In God, whose word I praise—in God I trust and am not afraid. What can mere mortals do to me?

Breath Prayer:

Begin with three slow, deep breaths. Pause briefly between each one. Then, for the next few minutes, prayerfully meditate on these phrases as you breathe:

- Inhale: *"When I am afraid,"*
- Exhale: *"I will trust in you."*

Listening Prayer:

I quiet my heart, turn my attention to Jesus, and simply listen. *What is God speaking to me through this Psalm and this time of meditation?*

Journal Reflection:

What did I sense during my breath or listening prayer? (Write freely here—thoughts, impressions, scriptures, images, or feelings.)

_____

_____

_____

_____

My "I Will" Statement:

How will I respond to this encounter with God's word? Whom can I share this with today?

_____

_____

> **Psalm 57:8-10**
> *Awake, my soul! Awake, harp and lyre! I will awaken the dawn. I will praise you, Lord, among the nations; I will sing of you among the peoples. For great is your love, reaching to the heavens; your faithfulness reaches to the skies.*

Breath Prayer:

Begin with three slow, deep breaths. Pause briefly between each one. Then, for the next few minutes, prayerfully meditate on these phrases as you breathe:

- Inhale: *"I awaken my soul to worship you,"*
- Exhale: *"for great is your love and faithfulness."*

Listening Prayer:

I quiet my heart, turn my attention to Jesus, and simply listen. *What is God speaking to me through this Psalm and this time of meditation?*

Journal Reflection:

What did I sense during my breath or listening prayer? (Write freely here—thoughts, impressions, scriptures, images, or feelings.)

_____
_____
_____
_____
_____

My "I Will" Statement:

How will I respond to this encounter with God's word? Whom can I share this with today?

_____
_____

Psalm 58:7

Let them vanish like water that flows away;
when they draw the bow, let their arrows fall short.

Breath Prayer:

Begin with three slow, deep breaths. Pause briefly between each one. Then, for the next few minutes, prayerfully meditate on these phrases as you breathe:

- Inhale: *"Lord, when the wicked draw the bow,"*
- Exhale: *"let their arrows fall short."*

Listening Prayer:

I quiet my heart, turn my attention to Jesus, and simply listen. *What is God speaking to me through this Psalm and this time of meditation?*

Journal Reflection:

What did I sense during my breath or listening prayer? (Write freely here—thoughts, impressions, scriptures, images, or feelings.)

_____
_____
_____
_____
_____

My "I Will" Statement:

How will I respond to this encounter with God's word? Whom can I share this with today?

_____
_____

Psalm 59:16-17	*But I will sing of your strength, in the morning I will sing of your love; for you are my fortress, my refuge in times of trouble. You are my strength, I sing praise to you; you, God, are my fortress, my God on whom I can rely.*

Breath Prayer:

Begin with three slow, deep breaths. Pause briefly between each one. Then, for the next few minutes, prayerfully meditate on these phrases as you breathe:

- Inhale: *"You are my strength and refuge"*
- Exhale: *"in times of trouble."*

Listening Prayer:

I quiet my heart, turn my attention to Jesus, and simply listen. *What is God speaking to me through this Psalm and this time of meditation?*

Journal Reflection:

What did I sense during my breath or listening prayer? (Write freely here—thoughts, impressions, scriptures, images, or feelings.)

_____
_____
_____
_____
_____

My "I Will" Statement:

How will I respond to this encounter with God's word? Whom can I share this with today?

_____
_____

Psalm 60:11-12

Give us aid against the enemy, for human help is worthless. With God we will gain the victory, and he will trample down our enemies.

Breath Prayer:

Begin with three slow, deep breaths. Pause briefly between each one. Then, for the next few minutes, prayerfully meditate on these phrases as you breathe:

- Inhale: *"With you, God, I will be victorious,"*
- Exhale: *"for you will overcome my foes."*

Listening Prayer:

I quiet my heart, turn my attention to Jesus, and simply listen. *What is God speaking to me through this Psalm and this time of meditation?*

Journal Reflection:

What did I sense during my breath or listening prayer? (Write freely here—thoughts, impressions, scriptures, images, or feelings.)

_____

_____

_____

_____

_____

My "I Will" Statement:

How will I respond to this encounter with God's word? Whom can I share this with today?

_____

_____

| Psalm 61:2 | *From the ends of the earth I call to you, I call as my heart grows faint; lead me to the rock that is higher than I. For you have been my refuge, a strong tower against the foe.* |

Breath Prayer:

Begin with three slow, deep breaths. Pause briefly between each one. Then, for the next few minutes, prayerfully meditate on these phrases as you breathe:

- Inhale: *"Lead me to the rock"*
- Exhale: *"that is higher than I."*

Listening Prayer:

I quiet my heart, turn my attention to Jesus, and simply listen. *What is God speaking to me through this Psalm and this time of meditation?*

Journal Reflection:

What did I sense during my breath or listening prayer? (Write freely here—thoughts, impressions, scriptures, images, or feelings.)

_____
_____
_____
_____
_____

My "I Will" Statement:

How will I respond to this encounter with God's word? Whom can I share this with today?

_____
_____

> **Psalm 62:5-8**
>
> *Yes, my soul, find rest in God; my hope comes from him. Truly he is my rock and my salvation; he is my fortress, I will not be shaken. My salvation and my honor depend on God; he is my mighty rock, my refuge. Trust in him at all times, you people; pour out your hearts to him, for God is our refuge.*

Breath Prayer:

Begin with three slow, deep breaths. Pause briefly between each one. Then, for the next few minutes, prayerfully meditate on these phrases as you breathe:

- Inhale: *"My soul finds rest in you, God;"*
- Exhale: *"my hope comes from you."*

Listening Prayer:

I quiet my heart, turn my attention to Jesus, and simply listen. *What is God speaking to me through this Psalm and this time of meditation?*

Journal Reflection:

What did I sense during my breath or listening prayer? (Write freely here—thoughts, impressions, scriptures, images, or feelings.)

_____

_____

_____

_____

_____

My "I Will" Statement:

How will I respond to this encounter with God's word? Whom can I share this with today?

_____

_____

Psalm 63:1

You, God, are my God, earnestly I seek you; I thirst for you, my whole being longs for you, in a dry and parched land where there is no water.

Breath Prayer:

Begin with three slow, deep breaths. Pause briefly between each one. Then, for the next few minutes, prayerfully meditate on these phrases as you breathe:

- Inhale: *"Earnestly I seek you, God;"*
- Exhale: *"I thirst for you in a dry and parched land."*

Listening Prayer:

I quiet my heart, turn my attention to Jesus, and simply listen. *What is God speaking to me through this Psalm and this time of meditation?*

Journal Reflection:

What did I sense during my breath or listening prayer? (Write freely here—thoughts, impressions, scriptures, images, or feelings.)

_____
_____
_____
_____

My "I Will" Statement:

How will I respond to this encounter with God's word? Whom can I share this with today?

_____
_____

| Psalm 64:9-10 | *All people will fear; they will proclaim the works of God and ponder what he has done. The righteous will rejoice in the LORD and take refuge in him; all the upright in heart will glory in him!* |

Breath Prayer:

Begin with three slow, deep breaths. Pause briefly between each one. Then, for the next few minutes, prayerfully meditate on these phrases as you breathe:

- Inhale: *"As I ponder what you have done,"*
- Exhale: *"help me proclaim your works, LORD."*

Listening Prayer:

I quiet my heart, turn my attention to Jesus, and simply listen. *What is God speaking to me through this Psalm and this time of meditation?*

Journal Reflection:

What did I sense during my breath or listening prayer? (Write freely here—thoughts, impressions, scriptures, images, or feelings.)

_____
_____
_____
_____

My "I Will" Statement:

How will I respond to this encounter with God's word? Whom can I share this with today?

_____
_____

> **Psalm 65:1-2**
>
> *Praise awaits you, our God, in Zion; to you our vows will be fulfilled. You who answer prayer, to you all people will come.*

Breath Prayer:

Begin with three slow, deep breaths. Pause briefly between each one. Then, for the next few minutes, prayerfully meditate on these phrases as you breathe:

- Inhale: *"I come to you now, my God,"*
- Exhale: *"to you who answers prayer."*

Listening Prayer:

I quiet my heart, turn my attention to Jesus, and simply listen. *What is God speaking to me through this Psalm and this time of meditation?*

Journal Reflection:

What did I sense during my breath or listening prayer? (Write freely here—thoughts, impressions, scriptures, images, or feelings.)

_____

_____

_____

_____

_____

My "I Will" Statement:

How will I respond to this encounter with God's word? Whom can I share this with today?

_____

_____

| Psalm 66:1-3 | *Shout for joy to God, all the earth! Sing the glory of his name; make his praise glorious. Say to God, "How awesome are your deeds! So great is your power that your enemies cringe before you."* |

Breath Prayer:

Begin with three slow, deep breaths. Pause briefly between each one. Then, for the next few minutes, prayerfully meditate on these phrases as you breathe:

- Inhale: *"God, your deeds are awesome,"*
- Exhale: *"and so great is your power!"*

Listening Prayer:

I quiet my heart, turn my attention to Jesus, and simply listen. *What is God speaking to me through this Psalm and this time of meditation?*

Journal Reflection:

What did I sense during my breath or listening prayer? (Write freely here—thoughts, impressions, scriptures, images, or feelings.)

_____

_____

_____

_____

My "I Will" Statement:

How will I respond to this encounter with God's word? Whom can I share this with today?

_____

_____

| Psalm 67:1-2 | *May God be gracious to us and bless us and make his face shine on us—so that your ways may be known on earth, your salvation among all nations.* |

Breath Prayer:

Begin with three slow, deep breaths. Pause briefly between each one. Then, for the next few minutes, prayerfully meditate on these phrases as you breathe:

- Inhale: *"God, be gracious to me and bless me"*
- Exhale: *"and make your face shine upon me."*

Listening Prayer:

I quiet my heart, turn my attention to Jesus, and simply listen. *What is God speaking to me through this Psalm and this time of meditation?*

Journal Reflection:

What did I sense during my breath or listening prayer? (Write freely here—thoughts, impressions, scriptures, images, or feelings.)

_____

_____

_____

_____

_____

My "I Will" Statement:

How will I respond to this encounter with God's word? Whom can I share this with today?

_____

_____

Psalm 68:28

Summon your power, God; show us your strength, our God, as you have done before.

Breath Prayer:

Begin with three slow, deep breaths. Pause briefly between each one. Then, for the next few minutes, prayerfully meditate on these phrases as you breathe:

- Inhale: *"Manifest your power, God,"*
- Exhale: *"as you have done before."*

Listening Prayer:

I quiet my heart, turn my attention to Jesus, and simply listen. *What is God speaking to me through this Psalm and this time of meditation?*

Journal Reflection:

What did I sense during my breath or listening prayer? (Write freely here—thoughts, impressions, scriptures, images, or feelings.)

_____
_____
_____
_____
_____

My "I Will" Statement:

How will I respond to this encounter with God's word? Whom can I share this with today?

_____
_____

Psalm 69:13-14

But I pray to you, LORD, in the time of your favor; in your great love, O God, answer me with your sure salvation. Rescue me from the mire, do not let me sink; deliver me from those who hate me, from the deep waters.

Breath Prayer:

Begin with three slow, deep breaths. Pause briefly between each one. Then, for the next few minutes, prayerfully meditate on these phrases as you breathe:

- Inhale: *"As I pray to you, LORD,"*
- Exhale: *"in your great love, answer me."*

Listening Prayer:

I quiet my heart, turn my attention to Jesus, and simply listen. *What is God speaking to me through this Psalm and this time of meditation?*

Journal Reflection:

What did I sense during my breath or listening prayer? (Write freely here—thoughts, impressions, scriptures, images, or feelings.)

_____

_____

_____

_____

My "I Will" Statement:

How will I respond to this encounter with God's word? Whom can I share this with today?

_____

_____

> **Psalm 70:5** — *But as for me, I am poor and needy; come quickly to me, O God. You are my help and my deliverer; LORD, do not delay.*

Breath Prayer:

Begin with three slow, deep breaths. Pause briefly between each one. Then, for the next few minutes, prayerfully meditate on these phrases as you breathe:

- Inhale: *"Come quickly to me, O God."*
- Exhale: *"You are my help and my deliverer."*

Listening Prayer:

I quiet my heart, turn my attention to Jesus, and simply listen. *What is God speaking to me through this Psalm and this time of meditation?*

Journal Reflection:

What did I sense during my breath or listening prayer? (Write freely here—thoughts, impressions, scriptures, images, or feelings.)

_____
_____
_____
_____
_____

My "I Will" Statement:

How will I respond to this encounter with God's word? Whom can I share this with today?

_____
_____

Psalm 71:14-15

As for me, I will always have hope; I will praise you more and more. My mouth will tell of your righteous deeds, of your saving acts all day long—though I know not how to relate them all.

Breath Prayer:

Begin with three slow, deep breaths. Pause briefly between each one. Then, for the next few minutes, prayerfully meditate on these phrases as you breathe:

- Inhale: *"I will always have hope in you;"*
- Exhale: *"I will praise you more and more."*

Listening Prayer:

I quiet my heart, turn my attention to Jesus, and simply listen. *What is God speaking to me through this Psalm and this time of meditation?*

Journal Reflection:

What did I sense during my breath or listening prayer? (Write freely here—thoughts, impressions, scriptures, images, or feelings.)

_____
_____
_____
_____

My "I Will" Statement:

How will I respond to this encounter with God's word? Whom can I share this with today?

_____
_____

Psalm 72:18-19

Praise be to the LORD God, the God of Israel, who alone does marvelous deeds. Praise be to his glorious name forever; may the whole earth be filled with his glory. Amen and Amen.

Breath Prayer:

Begin with three slow, deep breaths. Pause briefly between each one. Then, for the next few minutes, prayerfully meditate on these phrases as you breathe:

- Inhale: *"Praise be to your glorious name."*
- Exhale: *"May the whole earth be filled with your glory."*

Listening Prayer:

I quiet my heart, turn my attention to Jesus, and simply listen. *What is God speaking to me through this Psalm and this time of meditation?*

Journal Reflection:

What did I sense during my breath or listening prayer? (Write freely here—thoughts, impressions, scriptures, images, or feelings.)

_____

_____

_____

_____

_____

My "I Will" Statement:

How will I respond to this encounter with God's word? Whom can I share this with today?

_____

_____

| Psalm 73:25-26 | *Whom have I in heaven but you? And earth has nothing I desire besides you. My flesh and my heart may fail, but God is the strength of my heart and my portion forever.* |

Breath Prayer:

Begin with three slow, deep breaths. Pause briefly between each one. Then, for the next few minutes, prayerfully meditate on these phrases as you breathe:

- Inhale: *"Earth has nothing I desire"*
- Exhale: *"more than you."*

Listening Prayer:

I quiet my heart, turn my attention to Jesus, and simply listen. *What is God speaking to me through this Psalm and this time of meditation?*

Journal Reflection:

What did I sense during my breath or listening prayer? (Write freely here—thoughts, impressions, scriptures, images, or feelings.)

_____

_____

_____

_____

_____

My "I Will" Statement:

How will I respond to this encounter with God's word? Whom can I share this with today?

_____

_____

Psalm 74:16-17	*The day is yours, and yours also the night; you established the sun and moon. It was you who set all the boundaries of the earth; you made both summer and winter.*

Breath Prayer:

Begin with three slow, deep breaths. Pause briefly between each one. Then, for the next few minutes, prayerfully meditate on these phrases as you breathe:

- Inhale: *"The day is yours, and yours also the night;"*
- Exhale: *"you established the sun and moon."*

Listening Prayer:

I quiet my heart, turn my attention to Jesus, and simply listen. *What is God speaking to me through this Psalm and this time of meditation?*

Journal Reflection:

What did I sense during my breath or listening prayer? (Write freely here—thoughts, impressions, scriptures, images, or feelings.)

_____
_____
_____
_____
_____

My "I Will" Statement:

How will I respond to this encounter with God's word? Whom can I share this with today?

_____
_____

Psalm 75:1

We praise you, God, we praise you, for your Name is near; people tell of your wonderful deeds.

Breath Prayer:

Begin with three slow, deep breaths. Pause briefly between each one. Then, for the next few minutes, prayerfully meditate on these phrases as you breathe:

- Inhale: *"I praise you, oh wonder-working God,"*
- Exhale: *"I praise you, for you are near."*

Listening Prayer:

I quiet my heart, turn my attention to Jesus, and simply listen. *What is God speaking to me through this Psalm and this time of meditation?*

Journal Reflection:

What did I sense during my breath or listening prayer? (Write freely here—thoughts, impressions, scriptures, images, or feelings.)

_____

_____

_____

_____

My "I Will" Statement:

How will I respond to this encounter with God's word? Whom can I share this with today?

_____

_____

Psalm 76:4

*You are radiant with light,
more majestic than mountains rich with game.*

Breath Prayer:

Begin with three slow, deep breaths. Pause briefly between each one. Then, for the next few minutes, prayerfully meditate on these phrases as you breathe:

- Inhale: *"You are radiant with light,"*
- Exhale: *"more majestic than mountains rich with game."*

Listening Prayer:

I quiet my heart, turn my attention to Jesus, and simply listen. *What is God speaking to me through this Psalm and this time of meditation?*

Journal Reflection:

What did I sense during my breath or listening prayer? (Write freely here—thoughts, impressions, scriptures, images, or feelings.)

_____

_____

_____

_____

My "I Will" Statement:

How will I respond to this encounter with God's word? Whom can I share this with today?

_____

_____

| Psalm 77:11-12 | *I will remember the deeds of the LORD; yes, I will remember your miracles of long ago. I will consider all your works and meditate on all your mighty deeds.* |

Breath Prayer:

Begin with three slow, deep breaths. Pause briefly between each one. Then, for the next few minutes, prayerfully meditate on these phrases as you breathe:

- Inhale: *"I will remember your miracles"*
- Exhale: *"and meditate on your mighty deeds."*

Listening Prayer:

I quiet my heart, turn my attention to Jesus, and simply listen. *What is God speaking to me through this Psalm and this time of meditation?*

Journal Reflection:

What did I sense during my breath or listening prayer? (Write freely here—thoughts, impressions, scriptures, images, or feelings.)

_____
_____
_____
_____
_____

My "I Will" Statement:

How will I respond to this encounter with God's word? Whom can I share this with today?

_____
_____

| Psalm 78:2-4 | *I will utter hidden things, things from of old—things we have heard and known, things our ancestors have told us. We will not hide them from their descendants; we will tell the next generation the praiseworthy deeds of the LORD, his power, and the wonders he has done.* |

Breath Prayer:

Begin with three slow, deep breaths. Pause briefly between each one. Then, for the next few minutes, prayerfully meditate on these phrases as you breathe:

- Inhale: *"We will tell the next generation"*
- Exhale: *"the praiseworthy deeds that you have done."*

Listening Prayer:

I quiet my heart, turn my attention to Jesus, and simply listen. *What is God speaking to me through this Psalm and this time of meditation?*

Journal Reflection:

What did I sense during my breath or listening prayer? (Write freely here—thoughts, impressions, scriptures, images, or feelings.)

_____
_____
_____
_____
_____

My "I Will" Statement:

How will I respond to this encounter with God's word? Whom can I share this with today?

_____
_____

| Psalm 79:8-9 | *Do not hold against us the sins of past generations; may your mercy come quickly to meet us, for we are in desperate need. Help us, God our Savior, for the glory of your name; deliver us and forgive our sins for your name's sake.* |

Breath Prayer:

Begin with three slow, deep breaths. Pause briefly between each one. Then, for the next few minutes, prayerfully meditate on these phrases as you breathe:

- Inhale: *"Help me, God, for the glory of your name;"*
- Exhale: *"deliver me and forgive my sins."*

Listening Prayer:

I quiet my heart, turn my attention to Jesus, and simply listen. *What is God speaking to me through this Psalm and this time of meditation?*

Journal Reflection:

What did I sense during my breath or listening prayer? (Write freely here—thoughts, impressions, scriptures, images, or feelings.)

_____
_____
_____
_____

My "I Will" Statement:

How will I respond to this encounter with God's word? Whom can I share this with today?

_____
_____

Psalm 80:19

Restore us, LORD God Almighty; make your face shine on us, that we may be saved.

Breath Prayer:

Begin with three slow, deep breaths. Pause briefly between each one. Then, for the next few minutes, prayerfully meditate on these phrases as you breathe:

- Inhale: *"Restore me, LORD God Almighty;"*
- Exhale: *"make your face shine on me."*

Listening Prayer:

I quiet my heart, turn my attention to Jesus, and simply listen. *What is God speaking to me through this Psalm and this time of meditation?*

Journal Reflection:

What did I sense during my breath or listening prayer? (Write freely here—thoughts, impressions, scriptures, images, or feelings.)

_____

_____

_____

_____

My "I Will" Statement:

How will I respond to this encounter with God's word? Whom can I share this with today?

_____

_____

| Psalm 81:13-14 | *"If my people would only listen to me, if Israel would only follow my ways," how quickly I would subdue their enemies and turn my hand against their foes!* |

Breath Prayer:

Begin with three slow, deep breaths. Pause briefly between each one. Then, for the next few minutes, prayerfully meditate on these phrases as you breathe:

- Inhale: *"I will listen to you,"*
- Exhale: *"and follow your ways."*

Listening Prayer:

I quiet my heart, turn my attention to Jesus, and simply listen. *What is God speaking to me through this Psalm and this time of meditation?*

Journal Reflection:

What did I sense during my breath or listening prayer? (Write freely here—thoughts, impressions, scriptures, images, or feelings.)

_____

_____

_____

_____

My "I Will" Statement:

How will I respond to this encounter with God's word? Whom can I share this with today?

_____

_____

Psalm 82:3-4	*Defend the weak and the fatherless; uphold the cause of the poor and the oppressed. Rescue the weak and the needy; deliver them from the hand of the wicked.*

Breath Prayer:

Begin with three slow, deep breaths. Pause briefly between each one. Then, for the next few minutes, prayerfully meditate on these phrases as you breathe:

- Inhale: *"Help me defend the weak and the fatherless"*
- Exhale: *"and uphold the poor and the oppressed."*

Listening Prayer:

I quiet my heart, turn my attention to Jesus, and simply listen. *What is God speaking to me through this Psalm and this time of meditation?*

Journal Reflection:

What did I sense during my breath or listening prayer? (Write freely here—thoughts, impressions, scriptures, images, or feelings.)

_____

_____

_____

_____

_____

My "I Will" Statement:

How will I respond to this encounter with God's word? Whom can I share this with today?

_____

_____

Psalm 83:18

Let them know that you, whose name is the LORD — that you alone are the Most High over all the earth.

Breath Prayer:

Begin with three slow, deep breaths. Pause briefly between each one. Then, for the next few minutes, prayerfully meditate on these phrases as you breathe:

- Inhale: *"You alone, LORD,"*
- Exhale: *"are the Most High over all the earth."*

Listening Prayer:

I quiet my heart, turn my attention to Jesus, and simply listen. *What is God speaking to me through this Psalm and this time of meditation?*

Journal Reflection:

What did I sense during my breath or listening prayer? (Write freely here—thoughts, impressions, scriptures, images, or feelings.)

_____
_____
_____
_____
_____

My "I Will" Statement:

How will I respond to this encounter with God's word? Whom can I share this with today?

_____
_____

Psalm 84:10

Better is one day in your courts than a thousand elsewhere; I would rather be a doorkeeper in the house of my God than dwell in the tents of the wicked.

Breath Prayer:

Begin with three slow, deep breaths. Pause briefly between each one. Then, for the next few minutes, prayerfully meditate on these phrases as you breathe:

- Inhale: *"Better is one day in your presence"*
- Exhale: *"than a thousand elsewhere."*

Listening Prayer:

I quiet my heart, turn my attention to Jesus, and simply listen. *What is God speaking to me through this Psalm and this time of meditation?*

Journal Reflection:

What did I sense during my breath or listening prayer? (Write freely here—thoughts, impressions, scriptures, images, or feelings.)

_____

_____

_____

_____

_____

My "I Will" Statement:

How will I respond to this encounter with God's word? Whom can I share this with today?

_____

_____

Psalm 85:6-7

*Will you not revive us again,
that your people may rejoice in you?
Show us your unfailing love, LORD,
and grant us your salvation.*

Breath Prayer:

Begin with three slow, deep breaths. Pause briefly between each one. Then, for the next few minutes, prayerfully meditate on these phrases as you breathe:

- Inhale: *"Revive me again, LORD,"*
- Exhale: *"that I may rejoice in you."*

Listening Prayer:

I quiet my heart, turn my attention to Jesus, and simply listen. *What is God speaking to me through this Psalm and this time of meditation?*

Journal Reflection:

What did I sense during my breath or listening prayer? (Write freely here—thoughts, impressions, scriptures, images, or feelings.)

_____

_____

_____

_____

My "I Will" Statement:

How will I respond to this encounter with God's word? Whom can I share this with today?

_____

_____

| Psalm 86:2-4 | *Guard my life, for I am faithful to you; save your servant who trusts in you. You are my God; have mercy on me, Lord, for I call to you all day long. Bring joy to your servant, Lord, for I put my trust in you.* |

Breath Prayer:

Begin with three slow, deep breaths. Pause briefly between each one. Then, for the next few minutes, prayerfully meditate on these phrases as you breathe:

- Inhale: *"Bring joy to your servant, Lord,"*
- Exhale: *"for I put my trust in you."*

Listening Prayer:

I quiet my heart, turn my attention to Jesus, and simply listen. *What is God speaking to me through this Psalm and this time of meditation?*

Journal Reflection:

What did I sense during my breath or listening prayer? (Write freely here—thoughts, impressions, scriptures, images, or feelings.)

_____

_____

_____

_____

My "I Will" Statement:

How will I respond to this encounter with God's word? Whom can I share this with today?

_____

_____

Psalm 87:5, 7

*Indeed, of Zion it will be said, "This one and that one were born in her, and the Most High himself will establish her...."
As they make music they will sing,
"All my fountains are in you."*

Breath Prayer:

Begin with three slow, deep breaths. Pause briefly between each one. Then, for the next few minutes, prayerfully meditate on these phrases as you breathe:

- Inhale: *"You, God, will establish your Kingdom,"*
- Exhale: *"and I will sing, 'All my fountains are in you.'"*

Listening Prayer:

I quiet my heart, turn my attention to Jesus, and simply listen. *What is God speaking to me through this Psalm and this time of meditation?*

Journal Reflection:

What did I sense during my breath or listening prayer? (Write freely here—thoughts, impressions, scriptures, images, or feelings.)

_____
_____
_____
_____

My "I Will" Statement:

How will I respond to this encounter with God's word? Whom can I share this with today?

_____
_____

> **Psalm 88:1-2**
>
> *LORD, you are the God who saves me; day and night I cry out to you. May my prayer come before you; turn your ear to my cry.*

Breath Prayer:

Begin with three slow, deep breaths. Pause briefly between each one. Then, for the next few minutes, prayerfully meditate on these phrases as you breathe:

- Inhale: *"May my prayer come before you;"*
- Exhale: *"turn your ear to my cry."*

Listening Prayer:

I quiet my heart, turn my attention to Jesus, and simply listen. *What is God speaking to me through this Psalm and this time of meditation?*

Journal Reflection:

What did I sense during my breath or listening prayer? (Write freely here—thoughts, impressions, scriptures, images, or feelings.)

_____
_____
_____
_____

My "I Will" Statement:

How will I respond to this encounter with God's word? Whom can I share this with today?

_____
_____

Psalm 89:15-16

Blessed are those who have learned to acclaim you, who walk in the light of your presence, LORD. They rejoice in your name all day long; they celebrate your righteousness.

Breath Prayer:

Begin with three slow, deep breaths. Pause briefly between each one. Then, for the next few minutes, prayerfully meditate on these phrases as you breathe:

- Inhale: *"Help me walk in the light of your presence"*
- Exhale: *"and rejoice in your name all day long."*

Listening Prayer:

I quiet my heart, turn my attention to Jesus, and simply listen. *What is God speaking to me through this Psalm and this time of meditation?*

Journal Reflection:

What did I sense during my breath or listening prayer? (Write freely here—thoughts, impressions, scriptures, images, or feelings.)

_____
_____
_____
_____

My "I Will" Statement:

How will I respond to this encounter with God's word? Whom can I share this with today?

_____
_____

| Psalm 90:17 | *May the favor of the Lord our God rest on us; establish the work of our hands for us—yes, establish the work of our hands.* |

Breath Prayer:

Begin with three slow, deep breaths. Pause briefly between each one. Then, for the next few minutes, prayerfully meditate on these phrases as you breathe:

- Inhale: *"May your favor rest on me;"*
- Exhale: *"establish the work of my hands."*

Listening Prayer:

I quiet my heart, turn my attention to Jesus, and simply listen. *What is God speaking to me through this Psalm and this time of meditation?*

Journal Reflection:

What did I sense during my breath or listening prayer? (Write freely here—thoughts, impressions, scriptures, images, or feelings.)

_____

_____

_____

_____

My "I Will" Statement:

How will I respond to this encounter with God's word? Whom can I share this with today?

_____

_____

| Psalm 91:1-2 | *Whoever dwells in the shelter of the Most High will rest in the shadow of the Almighty. I will say of the LORD, "He is my refuge and my fortress, my God, in whom I trust."* |

Breath Prayer:

Begin with three slow, deep breaths. Pause briefly between each one. Then, for the next few minutes, prayerfully meditate on these phrases as you breathe:

- Inhale: *"Thank you for promising me rest,"*
- Exhale: *"as I dwell in the shadow of your presence."*

Listening Prayer:

I quiet my heart, turn my attention to Jesus, and simply listen. *What is God speaking to me through this Psalm and this time of meditation?*

Journal Reflection:

What did I sense during my breath or listening prayer? (Write freely here—thoughts, impressions, scriptures, images, or feelings.)

_____
_____
_____
_____

My "I Will" Statement:

How will I respond to this encounter with God's word? Whom can I share this with today?

_____
_____

Psalm 92:1-2, 5	*It is good to praise the LORD and make music to your name, O Most High, proclaiming your love in the morning and your faithfulness at night.... How great are your works, Lord, how profound your thoughts!*

Breath Prayer:

Begin with three slow, deep breaths. Pause briefly between each one. Then, for the next few minutes, prayerfully meditate on these phrases as you breathe:

- Inhale: *"How great are your works, LORD,"*
- Exhale: *"how profound your thoughts!"*

Listening Prayer:

I quiet my heart, turn my attention to Jesus, and simply listen. *What is God speaking to me through this Psalm and this time of meditation?*

Journal Reflection:

What did I sense during my breath or listening prayer? (Write freely here—thoughts, impressions, scriptures, images, or feelings.)

_____

_____

_____

_____

My "I Will" Statement:

How will I respond to this encounter with God's word? Whom can I share this with today?

_____

_____

> **Psalm 93:3-4**
>
> *The seas have lifted up, LORD, the seas have lifted up their voice; the seas have lifted up their pounding waves. Mightier than the thunder of the great waters, mightier than the breakers of the sea—the LORD on high is mighty.*

Breath Prayer:

Begin with three slow, deep breaths. Pause briefly between each one. Then, for the next few minutes, prayerfully meditate on these phrases as you breathe:

- Inhale: *"Mightier than the breakers of the sea—"*
- Exhale: *"you, the LORD on high, are mighty."*

Listening Prayer:

I quiet my heart, turn my attention to Jesus, and simply listen. *What is God speaking to me through this Psalm and this time of meditation?*

Journal Reflection:

What did I sense during my breath or listening prayer? (Write freely here—thoughts, impressions, scriptures, images, or feelings.)

_____
_____
_____
_____

My "I Will" Statement:

How will I respond to this encounter with God's word? Whom can I share this with today?

_____
_____

Psalm 94:18-19

When I said, "My foot is slipping," your unfailing love, LORD, supported me. When anxiety was great within me, your consolation brought me joy.

Breath Prayer:

Begin with three slow, deep breaths. Pause briefly between each one. Then, for the next few minutes, prayerfully meditate on these phrases as you breathe:

- Inhale: *"When anxiety is great within me,"*
- Exhale: *"help me trust in your unfailing love."*

Listening Prayer:

I quiet my heart, turn my attention to Jesus, and simply listen. *What is God speaking to me through this Psalm and this time of meditation?*

Journal Reflection:

What did I sense during my breath or listening prayer? (Write freely here—thoughts, impressions, scriptures, images, or feelings.)

_____

_____

_____

_____

My "I Will" Statement:

How will I respond to this encounter with God's word? Whom can I share this with today?

_____

_____

> **Psalm 95:6-7**
>
> *Come, let us bow down in worship, let us kneel before the LORD our Maker; for he is our God and we are the people of his pasture, the flock under his care.*

Breath Prayer:

Begin with three slow, deep breaths. Pause briefly between each one. Then, for the next few minutes, prayerfully meditate on these phrases as you breathe:

- Inhale: *"I will bow down in worship"*
- Exhale: *"for you are my God."*

Listening Prayer:

I quiet my heart, turn my attention to Jesus, and simply listen. *What is God speaking to me through this Psalm and this time of meditation?*

Journal Reflection:

What did I sense during my breath or listening prayer? (Write freely here—thoughts, impressions, scriptures, images, or feelings.)

_____
_____
_____
_____
_____

My "I Will" Statement:

How will I respond to this encounter with God's word? Whom can I share this with today?

_____
_____

| Psalm 96:3-4 | *Declare his glory among the nations, his marvelous deeds among all peoples. For great is the LORD and most worthy of praise; he is to be feared above all gods.* |

Breath Prayer:

Begin with three slow, deep breaths. Pause briefly between each one. Then, for the next few minutes, prayerfully meditate on these phrases as you breathe:

- Inhale: *"Great are you, LORD,"*
- Exhale: *"and most worthy of praise."*

Listening Prayer:

I quiet my heart, turn my attention to Jesus, and simply listen. *What is God speaking to me through this Psalm and this time of meditation?*

Journal Reflection:

What did I sense during my breath or listening prayer? (Write freely here—thoughts, impressions, scriptures, images, or feelings.)

_____
_____
_____
_____

My "I Will" Statement:

How will I respond to this encounter with God's word? Whom can I share this with today?

_____
_____

Psalm 97:11-12

Light shines on the righteous and joy on the upright in heart. Rejoice in the LORD, you who are righteous, and praise his holy name.

Breath Prayer:

Begin with three slow, deep breaths. Pause briefly between each one. Then, for the next few minutes, prayerfully meditate on these phrases as you breathe:

- Inhale: *"I rejoice in you and praise your name,"*
- Exhale: *"for you cover me with light and fill me with joy."*

Listening Prayer:

I quiet my heart, turn my attention to Jesus, and simply listen. *What is God speaking to me through this Psalm and this time of meditation?*

Journal Reflection:

What did I sense during my breath or listening prayer? (Write freely here—thoughts, impressions, scriptures, images, or feelings.)

_____
_____
_____
_____
_____

My "I Will" Statement:

How will I respond to this encounter with God's word? Whom can I share this with today?

_____
_____

Psalm 98:1

Sing to the LORD a new song, for he has done marvelous things; his right hand and his holy arm have worked salvation for him.

Breath Prayer:

Begin with three slow, deep breaths. Pause briefly between each one. Then, for the next few minutes, prayerfully meditate on these phrases as you breathe:

- Inhale: *"I will sing to you a new song,"*
- Exhale: *"for you have done marvelous things."*

Listening Prayer:

I quiet my heart, turn my attention to Jesus, and simply listen. *What is God speaking to me through this Psalm and this time of meditation?*

Journal Reflection:

What did I sense during my breath or listening prayer? (Write freely here—thoughts, impressions, scriptures, images, or feelings.)

_____

_____

_____

_____

My "I Will" Statement:

How will I respond to this encounter with God's word? Whom can I share this with today?

_____

_____

Psalm 99:4-5

The King is mighty, he loves justice—you have established equity; in Jacob you have done what is just and right. Exalt the LORD our God and worship at his footstool; he is holy.

Breath Prayer:

Begin with three slow, deep breaths. Pause briefly between each one. Then, for the next few minutes, prayerfully meditate on these phrases as you breathe:

- Inhale: *"I exalt you, my holy God,"*
- Exhale: *"and worship at your footstool."*

Listening Prayer:

I quiet my heart, turn my attention to Jesus, and simply listen. *What is God speaking to me through this Psalm and this time of meditation?*

Journal Reflection:

What did I sense during my breath or listening prayer? (Write freely here—thoughts, impressions, scriptures, images, or feelings.)

_____

_____

_____

_____

My "I Will" Statement:

How will I respond to this encounter with God's word? Whom can I share this with today?

_____

_____

| Psalm 100:4-5 | *Enter his gates with thanksgiving and his courts with praise; give thanks to him and praise his name. For the LORD is good and his love endures forever; his faithfulness continues through all generations.* |

Breath Prayer:

Begin with three slow, deep breaths. Pause briefly between each one. Then, for the next few minutes, prayerfully meditate on these phrases as you breathe:

- Inhale: *"I worship you, LORD, for you are good,"*
- Exhale: *"and your love endures forever."*

Listening Prayer:

I quiet my heart, turn my attention to Jesus, and simply listen. *What is God speaking to me through this Psalm and this time of meditation?*

Journal Reflection:

What did I sense during my breath or listening prayer? (Write freely here—thoughts, impressions, scriptures, images, or feelings.)

_____
_____
_____
_____

My "I Will" Statement:

How will I respond to this encounter with God's word? Whom can I share this with today?

_____
_____

| **Psalm 101:1-2** | *I will sing of your love and justice; to you, LORD, I will sing praise. I will be careful to lead a blameless life— when will you come to me?* |

Breath Prayer:

Begin with three slow, deep breaths. Pause briefly between each one. Then, for the next few minutes, prayerfully meditate on these phrases as you breathe:

- Inhale: *"I will sing of your love and justice,"*
- Exhale: *"and seek to lead a blameless life."*

Listening Prayer:

I quiet my heart, turn my attention to Jesus, and simply listen. *What is God speaking to me through this Psalm and this time of meditation?*

Journal Reflection:

What did I sense during my breath or listening prayer? (Write freely here—thoughts, impressions, scriptures, images, or feelings.)

_____

_____

_____

_____

_____

My "I Will" Statement:

How will I respond to this encounter with God's word? Whom can I share this with today?

_____

_____

Psalm 102:18

Let this be written for a future generation, that a people not yet created may praise the LORD.

Breath Prayer:

Begin with three slow, deep breaths. Pause briefly between each one. Then, for the next few minutes, prayerfully meditate on these phrases as you breathe:

- Inhale: *"I lift my prayers for a future generation,"*
- Exhale: *"that a people not yet created may praise you, LORD."*

Listening Prayer:

I quiet my heart, turn my attention to Jesus, and simply listen. *What is God speaking to me through this Psalm and this time of meditation?*

Journal Reflection:

What did I sense during my breath or listening prayer? (Write freely here—thoughts, impressions, scriptures, images, or feelings.)

_____
_____
_____
_____
_____

My "I Will" Statement:

How will I respond to this encounter with God's word? Whom can I share this with today?

_____
_____

| Psalm 103:8, 11-12 | *The LORD is compassionate and gracious, slow to anger, abounding in love.... For as high as the heavens are above the earth, so great is his love for those who fear him; as far as the east is from the west, so far has he removed our transgressions from us.* |

Breath Prayer:

Begin with three slow, deep breaths. Pause briefly between each one. Then, for the next few minutes, prayerfully meditate on these phrases as you breathe:

- Inhale: *"Thank you for removing my transgressions from me"*
- Exhale: *"as far as the east is from the west."*

Listening Prayer:

I quiet my heart, turn my attention to Jesus, and simply listen. *What is God speaking to me through this Psalm and this time of meditation?*

Journal Reflection:

What did I sense during my breath or listening prayer? (Write freely here—thoughts, impressions, scriptures, images, or feelings.)

_____

_____

_____

_____

_____

My "I Will" Statement:

How will I respond to this encounter with God's word? Whom can I share this with today?

_____

_____

Psalm 104:33-34

I will sing to the LORD all my life; I will sing praise to my God as long as I live. May my meditation be pleasing to him, as I rejoice in the LORD.

Breath Prayer:

Begin with three slow, deep breaths. Pause briefly between each one. Then, for the next few minutes, prayerfully meditate on these phrases as you breathe:

- Inhale: *"May my meditation be pleasing to you"*
- Exhale: *"as I rejoice in you, LORD."*

Listening Prayer:

I quiet my heart, turn my attention to Jesus, and simply listen. *What is God speaking to me through this Psalm and this time of meditation?*

Journal Reflection:

What did I sense during my breath or listening prayer? (Write freely here—thoughts, impressions, scriptures, images, or feelings.)

_____
_____
_____
_____

My "I Will" Statement:

How will I respond to this encounter with God's word? Whom can I share this with today?

_____
_____

Psalm 105:1-4

Give praise to the LORD, proclaim his name; make known among the nations what he has done. Sing to him, sing praise to him; tell of all his wonderful acts. Glory in his holy name; let the hearts of those who seek the LORD rejoice. Look to the LORD and his strength; seek his face always.

Breath Prayer:

Begin with three slow, deep breaths. Pause briefly between each one. Then, for the next few minutes, prayerfully meditate on these phrases as you breathe:

- Inhale: *"I will look to you, LORD, and your strength;"*
- Exhale: *"I will seek your face always."*

Listening Prayer:

I quiet my heart, turn my attention to Jesus, and simply listen. *What is God speaking to me through this Psalm and this time of meditation?*

Journal Reflection:

What did I sense during my breath or listening prayer? (Write freely here—thoughts, impressions, scriptures, images, or feelings.)

_____
_____
_____
_____
_____

My "I Will" Statement:

How will I respond to this encounter with God's word? Whom can I share this with today?

_____
_____

Psalm 106:1-2

Praise the LORD. Give thanks to the LORD, for he is good; his love endures forever. Who can proclaim the mighty acts of the LORD or fully declare his praise?

Breath Prayer:

Begin with three slow, deep breaths. Pause briefly between each one. Then, for the next few minutes, prayerfully meditate on these phrases as you breathe:

- Inhale: *"I thank you, LORD, for you are good;"*
- Exhale: *"your love endures forever."*

Listening Prayer:

I quiet my heart, turn my attention to Jesus, and simply listen. *What is God speaking to me through this Psalm and this time of meditation?*

Journal Reflection:

What did I sense during my breath or listening prayer? (Write freely here—thoughts, impressions, scriptures, images, or feelings.)

_____

_____

_____

_____

My "I Will" Statement:

How will I respond to this encounter with God's word? Whom can I share this with today?

_____

_____

Psalm 107:8-9

Let them give thanks to the LORD for his unfailing love and his wonderful deeds for mankind, for he satisfies the thirsty and fills the hungry with good things.

Breath Prayer:

Begin with three slow, deep breaths. Pause briefly between each one. Then, for the next few minutes, prayerfully meditate on these phrases as you breathe:

- Inhale: *"You, LORD, satisfy the thirsty"*
- Exhale: *"and fill the hungry with good things."*

Listening Prayer:

I quiet my heart, turn my attention to Jesus, and simply listen. *What is God speaking to me through this Psalm and this time of meditation?*

Journal Reflection:

What did I sense during my breath or listening prayer? (Write freely here— thoughts, impressions, scriptures, images, or feelings.)

_____

_____

_____

_____

My "I Will" Statement:

How will I respond to this encounter with God's word? Whom can I share this with today?

_____

_____

| Psalm 108:3-5 | *I will praise you, LORD, among the nations; I will sing of you among the peoples. For great is your love, higher than the heavens; your faithfulness reaches to the skies. Be exalted, O God, above the heavens; let your glory be over all the earth.* |

Breath Prayer:

Begin with three slow, deep breaths. Pause briefly between each one. Then, for the next few minutes, prayerfully meditate on these phrases as you breathe:

- Inhale: *"Be exalted, O God, above the heavens;"*
- Exhale: *"let your glory be over all the earth."*

Listening Prayer:

I quiet my heart, turn my attention to Jesus, and simply listen. *What is God speaking to me through this Psalm and this time of meditation?*

Journal Reflection:

What did I sense during my breath or listening prayer? (Write freely here—thoughts, impressions, scriptures, images, or feelings.)

_____

_____

_____

_____

My "I Will" Statement:

How will I respond to this encounter with God's word? Whom can I share this with today?

_____

_____

| Psalm 109:21-22 | *But you, Sovereign LORD, help me for your name's sake; out of the goodness of your love, deliver me. For I am poor and needy, and my heart is wounded within me.* |

Breath Prayer:

Begin with three slow, deep breaths. Pause briefly between each one. Then, for the next few minutes, prayerfully meditate on these phrases as you breathe:

- Inhale: *"LORD, help me for I am poor and needy,"*
- Exhale: *"and my heart is wounded within me."*

Listening Prayer:

I quiet my heart, turn my attention to Jesus, and simply listen. *What is God speaking to me through this Psalm and this time of meditation?*

Journal Reflection:

What did I sense during my breath or listening prayer? (Write freely here—thoughts, impressions, scriptures, images, or feelings.)

_____

_____

_____

_____

My "I Will" Statement:

How will I respond to this encounter with God's word? Whom can I share this with today?

_____

_____

Psalm 110:5

*The Lord is at your right hand;
he will crush kings on the day of his wrath.*

Breath Prayer:

Begin with three slow, deep breaths. Pause briefly between each one. Then, for the next few minutes, prayerfully meditate on these phrases as you breathe:

- Inhale: *"I am grateful that you are with me"*
- Exhale: *"and will crush the evil rulers among the nations."*

Listening Prayer:

I quiet my heart, turn my attention to Jesus, and simply listen. *What is God speaking to me through this Psalm and this time of meditation?*

Journal Reflection:

What did I sense during my breath or listening prayer? (Write freely here—thoughts, impressions, scriptures, images, or feelings.)

_____

_____

_____

_____

My "I Will" Statement:

How will I respond to this encounter with God's word? Whom can I share this with today?

_____

_____

Psalm 111:1-2

Praise the LORD. I will extol the LORD with all my heart in the council of the upright and in the assembly. Great are the works of the LORD; they are pondered by all who delight in them.

Breath Prayer:

Begin with three slow, deep breaths. Pause briefly between each one. Then, for the next few minutes, prayerfully meditate on these phrases as you breathe:

- Inhale: *"I will extol you, LORD, with all my heart"*
- Exhale: *"and delight in your great works."*

Listening Prayer:

I quiet my heart, turn my attention to Jesus, and simply listen. *What is God speaking to me through this Psalm and this time of meditation?*

Journal Reflection:

What did I sense during my breath or listening prayer? (Write freely here—thoughts, impressions, scriptures, images, or feelings.)

_____
_____
_____
_____
_____

My "I Will" Statement:

How will I respond to this encounter with God's word? Whom can I share this with today?

_____
_____

Psalm 112:1, 7-8	*Praise the LORD. Blessed are those who fear the LORD, who find great delight in his commands... They will have no fear of bad news; their hearts are steadfast, trusting in the Lord. Their hearts are secure...*

Breath Prayer:

Begin with three slow, deep breaths. Pause briefly between each one. Then, for the next few minutes, prayerfully meditate on these phrases as you breathe:

- Inhale: *"You make me fearless, steadfast and secure"*
- Exhale: *"as I live in awe of you and delight in your commands."*

Listening Prayer:

I quiet my heart, turn my attention to Jesus, and simply listen. *What is God speaking to me through this Psalm and this time of meditation?*

Journal Reflection:

What did I sense during my breath or listening prayer? (Write freely here—thoughts, impressions, scriptures, images, or feelings.)

_____
_____
_____
_____
_____

My "I Will" Statement:

How will I respond to this encounter with God's word? Whom can I share this with today?

_____
_____

> **Psalm 113:2-3**
>
> *Let the name of the LORD be praised, both now and forevermore. From the rising of the sun to the place where it sets, the name of the LORD is to be praised.*

Breath Prayer:

Begin with three slow, deep breaths. Pause briefly between each one. Then, for the next few minutes, prayerfully meditate on these phrases as you breathe:

- Inhale: *"From the rising of the sun to the place where it sets,"*
- Exhale: *"I will praise your name, O LORD."*

Listening Prayer:

I quiet my heart, turn my attention to Jesus, and simply listen. *What is God speaking to me through this Psalm and this time of meditation?*

Journal Reflection:

What did I sense during my breath or listening prayer? (Write freely here—thoughts, impressions, scriptures, images, or feelings.)

_____

_____

_____

_____

_____

My "I Will" Statement:

How will I respond to this encounter with God's word? Whom can I share this with today?

_____

_____

Psalm 114:7-8

Tremble, earth, at the presence of the Lord, at the presence of the God of Jacob, who turned the rock into a pool, the hard rock into springs of water.

Breath Prayer:

Begin with three slow, deep breaths. Pause briefly between each one. Then, for the next few minutes, prayerfully meditate on these phrases as you breathe:

- Inhale: *"May your presence turn my hard rocks"*
- Exhale: *"into springs of water."*

Listening Prayer:

I quiet my heart, turn my attention to Jesus, and simply listen. *What is God speaking to me through this Psalm and this time of meditation?*

Journal Reflection:

What did I sense during my breath or listening prayer? (Write freely here—thoughts, impressions, scriptures, images, or feelings.)

_____

_____

_____

_____

My "I Will" Statement:

How will I respond to this encounter with God's word? Whom can I share this with today?

_____

_____

| Psalm 115:14-15 | *May the LORD cause you to flourish, both you and your children. May you be blessed by the LORD, the Maker of heaven and earth.* |

Breath Prayer:

Begin with three slow, deep breaths. Pause briefly between each one. Then, for the next few minutes, prayerfully meditate on these phrases as you breathe:

- Inhale: *"May you bless both us and our children,"*
- Exhale: *"and cause us all to flourish."*

Listening Prayer:

I quiet my heart, turn my attention to Jesus, and simply listen. *What is God speaking to me through this Psalm and this time of meditation?*

Journal Reflection:

What did I sense during my breath or listening prayer? (Write freely here—thoughts, impressions, scriptures, images, or feelings.)

_____

_____

_____

_____

My "I Will" Statement:

How will I respond to this encounter with God's word? Whom can I share this with today?

_____

_____

Psalm 116:7-9

Return to your rest, my soul, for the LORD has been good to you. For you, LORD, have delivered me from death, my eyes from tears, my feet from stumbling, that I may walk before the LORD in the land of the living.

Breath Prayer:

Begin with three slow, deep breaths. Pause briefly between each one. Then, for the next few minutes, prayerfully meditate on these phrases as you breathe:

- Inhale: *"May my soul return to rest,"*
- Exhale: *"for you, LORD, have been good to me."*

Listening Prayer:

I quiet my heart, turn my attention to Jesus, and simply listen. *What is God speaking to me through this Psalm and this time of meditation?*

Journal Reflection:

What did I sense during my breath or listening prayer? (Write freely here—thoughts, impressions, scriptures, images, or feelings.)

_____

_____

_____

_____

_____

My "I Will" Statement:

How will I respond to this encounter with God's word? Whom can I share this with today?

_____

_____

Psalm 117:1-2

Praise the LORD, all you nations; extol him, all you peoples. For great is his love toward us, and the faithfulness of the LORD endures forever. Praise the LORD.

Breath Prayer:

Begin with three slow, deep breaths. Pause briefly between each one. Then, for the next few minutes, prayerfully meditate on these phrases as you breathe:

- Inhale: *"Great is your love toward me,"*
- Exhale: *"and your faithfulness endures forever."*

Listening Prayer:

I quiet my heart, turn my attention to Jesus, and simply listen. *What is God speaking to me through this Psalm and this time of meditation?*

Journal Reflection:

What did I sense during my breath or listening prayer? (Write freely here—thoughts, impressions, scriptures, images, or feelings.)

_____
_____
_____
_____
_____

My "I Will" Statement:

How will I respond to this encounter with God's word? Whom can I share this with today?

_____
_____

| Psalm 118:5-7 | *When hard pressed, I cried to the LORD; he brought me into a spacious place. The LORD is with me; I will not be afraid. What can mere mortals do to me? The LORD is with me; he is my helper. I look in triumph on my enemies.* |

Breath Prayer:

Begin with three slow, deep breaths. Pause briefly between each one. Then, for the next few minutes, prayerfully meditate on these phrases as you breathe:

- Inhale: *"LORD, you are with me;"*
- Exhale: *"I will not be afraid."*

Listening Prayer:

I quiet my heart, turn my attention to Jesus, and simply listen. *What is God speaking to me through this Psalm and this time of meditation?*

Journal Reflection:

What did I sense during my breath or listening prayer? (Write freely here—thoughts, impressions, scriptures, images, or feelings.)

_____
_____
_____
_____

My "I Will" Statement:

How will I respond to this encounter with God's word? Whom can I share this with today?

_____
_____

| Psalm 119:43-45 | *Never take your word of truth from my mouth, for I have put my hope in your laws. I will always obey your law, for ever and ever. I will walk about in freedom, for I have sought out your precepts.* |

Breath Prayer:

Begin with three slow, deep breaths. Pause briefly between each one. Then, for the next few minutes, prayerfully meditate on these phrases as you breathe:

- Inhale: *"I will walk about in freedom,"*
- Exhale: *"for I have sought out your precepts."*

Listening Prayer:

I quiet my heart, turn my attention to Jesus, and simply listen. *What is God speaking to me through this Psalm and this time of meditation?*

Journal Reflection:

What did I sense during my breath or listening prayer? (Write freely here—thoughts, impressions, scriptures, images, or feelings.)

_____
_____
_____
_____
_____

My "I Will" Statement:

How will I respond to this encounter with God's word? Whom can I share this with today?

_____
_____

Psalm 120:1-2

I call on the LORD in my distress, and he answers me. Save me, LORD, from lying lips and from deceitful tongues.

Breath Prayer:

Begin with three slow, deep breaths. Pause briefly between each one. Then, for the next few minutes, prayerfully meditate on these phrases as you breathe:

- Inhale: *"I call on you, LORD, in my distress,"*
- Exhale: *"and you answer me."*

Listening Prayer:

I quiet my heart, turn my attention to Jesus, and simply listen. *What is God speaking to me through this Psalm and this time of meditation?*

Journal Reflection:

What did I sense during my breath or listening prayer? (Write freely here—thoughts, impressions, scriptures, images, or feelings.)

_____

_____

_____

_____

_____

My "I Will" Statement:

How will I respond to this encounter with God's word? Whom can I share this with today?

_____

_____

Psalm 121:7-8	*The LORD will keep you from all harm—he will watch over your life; the LORD will watch over your coming and going both now and forevermore.*

Breath Prayer:

Begin with three slow, deep breaths. Pause briefly between each one. Then, for the next few minutes, prayerfully meditate on these phrases as you breathe:

- Inhale: *"You always watch over"*
- Exhale: *"my coming and going."*

Listening Prayer:

I quiet my heart, turn my attention to Jesus, and simply listen. *What is God speaking to me through this Psalm and this time of meditation?*

Journal Reflection:

What did I sense during my breath or listening prayer? (Write freely here—thoughts, impressions, scriptures, images, or feelings.)

_____

_____

_____

_____

My "I Will" Statement:

How will I respond to this encounter with God's word? Whom can I share this with today?

_____

_____

Psalm 122:1-2

I rejoiced with those who said to me, "Let us go to the house of the LORD." Our feet are standing in your gates, Jerusalem.

Breath Prayer:

Begin with three slow, deep breaths. Pause briefly between each one. Then, for the next few minutes, prayerfully meditate on these phrases as you breathe:

- Inhale: *"I rejoice as I go"*
- Exhale: *"to meet with you, LORD."*

Listening Prayer:

I quiet my heart, turn my attention to Jesus, and simply listen. *What is God speaking to me through this Psalm and this time of meditation?*

Journal Reflection:

What did I sense during my breath or listening prayer? (Write freely here—thoughts, impressions, scriptures, images, or feelings.)

_____

_____

_____

_____

_____

My "I Will" Statement:

How will I respond to this encounter with God's word? Whom can I share this with today?

_____

_____

> **Psalm 123:2**
>
> *As the eyes of slaves look to the hand of their master, as the eyes of a female slave look to the hand of her mistress, so our eyes look to the LORD our God, till he shows us his mercy.*

Breath Prayer:

Begin with three slow, deep breaths. Pause briefly between each one. Then, for the next few minutes, prayerfully meditate on these phrases as you breathe:

- Inhale: *"My eyes are fixed on you;"*
- Exhale: *"please show me your mercy."*

Listening Prayer:

I quiet my heart, turn my attention to Jesus, and simply listen. *What is God speaking to me through this Psalm and this time of meditation?*

Journal Reflection:

What did I sense during my breath or listening prayer? (Write freely here—thoughts, impressions, scriptures, images, or feelings.)

_____
_____
_____
_____
_____

My "I Will" Statement:

How will I respond to this encounter with God's word? Whom can I share this with today?

_____
_____

| Psalm 124:1-3, 8 | *If the LORD had not been on our side—let Israel say—if the LORD had not been on our side when people attacked us, they would have swallowed us alive.... Our help is in the name of the LORD, the Maker of heaven and earth.* |

Breath Prayer:

Begin with three slow, deep breaths. Pause briefly between each one. Then, for the next few minutes, prayerfully meditate on these phrases as you breathe:

- Inhale: *"My help is in your name, LORD,"*
- Exhale: *"the Maker of heaven and earth."*

Listening Prayer:

I quiet my heart, turn my attention to Jesus, and simply listen. *What is God speaking to me through this Psalm and this time of meditation?*

Journal Reflection:

What did I sense during my breath or listening prayer? (Write freely here—thoughts, impressions, scriptures, images, or feelings.)

_____

_____

_____

_____

_____

My "I Will" Statement:

How will I respond to this encounter with God's word? Whom can I share this with today?

_____

_____

| **Psalm 125:1-2** | *Those who trust in the LORD are like Mount Zion, which cannot be shaken but endures forever. As the mountains surround Jerusalem, so the LORD surrounds his people both now and forevermore.* |

Breath Prayer:

Begin with three slow, deep breaths. Pause briefly between each one. Then, for the next few minutes, prayerfully meditate on these phrases as you breathe:

- Inhale: *"Thank you for surrounding me,"*
- Exhale: *"both now and forever."*

Listening Prayer:

I quiet my heart, turn my attention to Jesus, and simply listen. *What is God speaking to me through this Psalm and this time of meditation?*

Journal Reflection:

What did I sense during my breath or listening prayer? (Write freely here—thoughts, impressions, scriptures, images, or feelings.)

_____
_____
_____
_____

My "I Will" Statement:

How will I respond to this encounter with God's word? Whom can I share this with today?

_____
_____

> **Psalm 126:5-6**
>
> *Those who sow with tears will reap with songs of joy. Those who go out weeping, carrying seed to sow, will return with songs of joy, carrying sheaves with them.*

Breath Prayer:

Begin with three slow, deep breaths. Pause briefly between each one. Then, for the next few minutes, prayerfully meditate on these phrases as you breathe:

- Inhale: *"Thank you, that when I sow tears,"*
- Exhale: *"I will eventually reap songs of joy."*

Listening Prayer:

I quiet my heart, turn my attention to Jesus, and simply listen. *What is God speaking to me through this Psalm and this time of meditation?*

Journal Reflection:

What did I sense during my breath or listening prayer? (Write freely here—thoughts, impressions, scriptures, images, or feelings.)

_____

_____

_____

_____

_____

My "I Will" Statement:

How will I respond to this encounter with God's word? Whom can I share this with today?

_____

_____

| Psalm 127:1-2 | *Unless the LORD builds the house, the builders labor in vain. Unless the LORD watches over the city, the guards stand watch in vain. In vain you rise early and stay up late, toiling for food to eat—for he grants sleep to those he loves.* |

Breath Prayer:

Begin with three slow, deep breaths. Pause briefly between each one. Then, for the next few minutes, prayerfully meditate on these phrases as you breathe:

- Inhale: *"Unless you, LORD, are the builder,"*
- Exhale: *"my labor will be in vain."*

Listening Prayer:

I quiet my heart, turn my attention to Jesus, and simply listen. *What is God speaking to me through this Psalm and this time of meditation?*

Journal Reflection:

What did I sense during my breath or listening prayer? (Write freely here—thoughts, impressions, scriptures, images, or feelings.)

___

___

___

___

___

My "I Will" Statement:

How will I respond to this encounter with God's word? Whom can I share this with today?

___

___

| Psalm 128:1-2 | *Blessed are all who fear the LORD, who walk in obedience to him. You will eat the fruit of your labor; blessings and prosperity will be yours.* |

Breath Prayer:

Begin with three slow, deep breaths. Pause briefly between each one. Then, for the next few minutes, prayerfully meditate on these phrases as you breathe:

- Inhale: *"I am blessed as I live in awe of you"*
- Exhale: *"and walk in obedience to your lead."*

Listening Prayer:

I quiet my heart, turn my attention to Jesus, and simply listen. *What is God speaking to me through this Psalm and this time of meditation?*

Journal Reflection:

What did I sense during my breath or listening prayer? (Write freely here—thoughts, impressions, scriptures, images, or feelings.)

_____

_____

_____

_____

_____

My "I Will" Statement:

How will I respond to this encounter with God's word? Whom can I share this with today?

_____

_____

| Psalm 129:3-4 | *Plowmen have plowed my back and made their furrows long. But the LORD is righteous; he has cut me free from the cords of the wicked.* |

Breath Prayer:
Begin with three slow, deep breaths. Pause briefly between each one. Then, for the next few minutes, prayerfully meditate on these phrases as you breathe:

- Inhale: *"You are righteous, LORD,"*
- Exhale: *"and have set me free."*

Listening Prayer:
I quiet my heart, turn my attention to Jesus, and simply listen. *What is God speaking to me through this Psalm and this time of meditation?*

Journal Reflection:
What did I sense during my breath or listening prayer? (Write freely here—thoughts, impressions, scriptures, images, or feelings.)

_____
_____
_____
_____
_____

My "I Will" Statement:
How will I respond to this encounter with God's word? Whom can I share this with today?

_____
_____

Psalm 130:5-6	*I wait for the LORD, my whole being waits, and in his word I put my hope. I wait for the Lord more than watchmen wait for the morning, more than watchmen wait for the morning.*

Breath Prayer:

Begin with three slow, deep breaths. Pause briefly between each one. Then, for the next few minutes, prayerfully meditate on these phrases as you breathe:

- Inhale: *"I wait for you, LORD,"*
- Exhale: *"and in your word I put my hope."*

Listening Prayer:

I quiet my heart, turn my attention to Jesus, and simply listen. *What is God speaking to me through this Psalm and this time of meditation?*

Journal Reflection:

What did I sense during my breath or listening prayer? (Write freely here—thoughts, impressions, scriptures, images, or feelings.)

_____

_____

_____

My "I Will" Statement:

How will I respond to this encounter with God's word? Whom can I share this with today?

_____

_____

| Psalm 131:1-2 | *My heart is not proud, LORD, my eyes are not haughty; I do not concern myself with great matters or things too wonderful for me. But I have calmed and quieted myself, I am like a weaned child with its mother; like a weaned child I am content.* |

Breath Prayer:

Begin with three slow, deep breaths. Pause briefly between each one. Then, for the next few minutes, prayerfully meditate on these phrases as you breathe:

- Inhale: *"I have calmed and quieted my soul;"*
- Exhale: *"like a weaned child with his mother, I am content."*

Listening Prayer:

I quiet my heart, turn my attention to Jesus, and simply listen. *What is God speaking to me through this Psalm and this time of meditation?*

Journal Reflection:

What did I sense during my breath or listening prayer? (Write freely here—thoughts, impressions, scriptures, images, or feelings.)

_____
_____
_____
_____
_____

My "I Will" Statement:

How will I respond to this encounter with God's word? Whom can I share this with today?

_____
_____

Psalm 132:3-5	*I will not enter my house or go to my bed, I will allow no sleep to my eyes or slumber to my eyelids, till I find a place for the LORD, a dwelling for the Mighty One of Jacob.*

Breath Prayer:

Begin with three slow, deep breaths. Pause briefly between each one. Then, for the next few minutes, prayerfully meditate on these phrases as you breathe:

- Inhale: *"I set apart my heart and mind"*
- Exhale: *"to be a dwelling place for you."*

Listening Prayer:

I quiet my heart, turn my attention to Jesus, and simply listen. *What is God speaking to me through this Psalm and this time of meditation?*

Journal Reflection:

What did I sense during my breath or listening prayer? (Write freely here—thoughts, impressions, scriptures, images, or feelings.)

_____

_____

_____

_____

My "I Will" Statement:

How will I respond to this encounter with God's word? Whom can I share this with today?

_____

_____

Psalm 133:1-3	*How good and pleasant it is when God's people live together in unity! It is like precious oil poured on the head, running down on the beard, running down on Aaron's beard, down on the collar of his robe. It is as if the dew of Hermon were falling on Mount Zion. For there the LORD bestows his blessing, even life forevermore.*

Breath Prayer:

Begin with three slow, deep breaths. Pause briefly between each one. Then, for the next few minutes, prayerfully meditate on these phrases as you breathe:

- Inhale: *"LORD, unify your people,"*
- Exhale: *"for this is where you bestow your blessing."*

Listening Prayer:

I quiet my heart, turn my attention to Jesus, and simply listen. *What is God speaking to me through this Psalm and this time of meditation?*

Journal Reflection:

What did I sense during my breath or listening prayer? (Write freely here—thoughts, impressions, scriptures, images, or feelings.)

_____

_____

_____

_____

My "I Will" Statement:

How will I respond to this encounter with God's word? Whom can I share this with today?

_____

_____

> **Psalm 134:1-2**
>
> *Praise the LORD, all you servants of the LORD who minister by night in the house of the LORD. Lift up your hands in the sanctuary and praise the LORD.*

Breath Prayer:

Begin with three slow, deep breaths. Pause briefly between each one. Then, for the next few minutes, prayerfully meditate on these phrases as you breathe:

- Inhale: *"I lift my hands in your presence"*
- Exhale: *"and praise you, LORD."*

Listening Prayer:

I quiet my heart, turn my attention to Jesus, and simply listen. *What is God speaking to me through this Psalm and this time of meditation?*

Journal Reflection:

What did I sense during my breath or listening prayer? (Write freely here—thoughts, impressions, scriptures, images, or feelings.)

_____

_____

_____

_____

My "I Will" Statement:

How will I respond to this encounter with God's word? Whom can I share this with today?

_____

_____

> **Psalm 135:5-7**
>
> *I know that the LORD is great, that our Lord is greater than all gods. The LORD does whatever pleases him, in the heavens and on the earth, in the seas and all their depths. He makes clouds rise from the ends of the earth; he sends lightning with the rain and brings out the wind from his storehouses.*

Breath Prayer:

Begin with three slow, deep breaths. Pause briefly between each one. Then, for the next few minutes, prayerfully meditate on these phrases as you breathe:

- Inhale: *"LORD, you are great,"*
- Exhale: *"greater than all gods."*

Listening Prayer:

I quiet my heart, turn my attention to Jesus, and simply listen. *What is God speaking to me through this Psalm and this time of meditation?*

Journal Reflection:

What did I sense during my breath or listening prayer? (Write freely here—thoughts, impressions, scriptures, images, or feelings.)

_____
_____
_____
_____
_____

My "I Will" Statement:

How will I respond to this encounter with God's word? Whom can I share this with today?

_____
_____

> **Psalm 136:1-3**
>
> *Give thanks to the LORD, for he is good. His love endures forever.*
> *Give thanks to the God of gods. His love endures forever.*
> *Give thanks to the Lord of lords:*
> *His love endures forever.*

Breath Prayer:

Begin with three slow, deep breaths. Pause briefly between each one. Then, for the next few minutes, prayerfully meditate on these phrases as you breathe:

- Inhale: *"I thank you, LORD, for you are good,"*
- Exhale: *"and your love never fails."*

Listening Prayer:

I quiet my heart, turn my attention to Jesus, and simply listen. *What is God speaking to me through this Psalm and this time of meditation?*

Journal Reflection:

What did I sense during my breath or listening prayer? (Write freely here—thoughts, impressions, scriptures, images, or feelings.)

_____

_____

_____

_____

My "I Will" Statement:

How will I respond to this encounter with God's word? Whom can I share this with today?

_____

_____

| Psalm 137:4-6 | *How can we sing the songs of the LORD while in a foreign land? If I forget you, Jerusalem, may my right hand forget its skill. May my tongue cling to the roof of my mouth if I do not remember you, if I do not consider Jerusalem my highest joy.* |

Breath Prayer:

Begin with three slow, deep breaths. Pause briefly between each one. Then, for the next few minutes, prayerfully meditate on these phrases as you breathe:

- Inhale: *"I will not forget your chosen dwelling place"*
- Exhale: *"or that your presence is my highest joy."*

Listening Prayer:

I quiet my heart, turn my attention to Jesus, and simply listen. *What is God speaking to me through this Psalm and this time of meditation?*

Journal Reflection:

What did I sense during my breath or listening prayer? (Write freely here—thoughts, impressions, scriptures, images, or feelings.)

_____
_____
_____
_____

My "I Will" Statement:

How will I respond to this encounter with God's word? Whom can I share this with today?

_____
_____

| Psalm 138:6-7 | *Though the LORD is exalted, he looks kindly on the lowly; though lofty, he sees them from afar. Though I walk in the midst of trouble, you preserve my life. You stretch out your hand against the anger of my foes; with your right hand you save me.* |

Breath Prayer:

Begin with three slow, deep breaths. Pause briefly between each one. Then, for the next few minutes, prayerfully meditate on these phrases as you breathe:

- Inhale: *"In the midst of trouble,"*
- Exhale: *"you preserve my life."*

Listening Prayer:

I quiet my heart, turn my attention to Jesus, and simply listen. *What is God speaking to me through this Psalm and this time of meditation?*

Journal Reflection:

What did I sense during my breath or listening prayer? (Write freely here—thoughts, impressions, scriptures, images, or feelings.)

_____
_____
_____
_____
_____

My "I Will" Statement:

How will I respond to this encounter with God's word? Whom can I share this with today?

_____
_____

> **Psalm 139:3-6**
>
> *You discern my going out and my lying down; you are familiar with all my ways. Before a word is on my tongue you, LORD, know it completely. You hem me in behind and before, and you lay your hand upon me. Such knowledge is too wonderful for me, too lofty for me to attain.*

Breath Prayer:

Begin with three slow, deep breaths. Pause briefly between each one. Then, for the next few minutes, prayerfully meditate on these phrases as you breathe:

- Inhale: *"Thank you for encircling me"*
- Exhale: *"and laying your hand upon me."*

Listening Prayer:

I quiet my heart, turn my attention to Jesus, and simply listen. *What is God speaking to me through this Psalm and this time of meditation?*

Journal Reflection:

What did I sense during my breath or listening prayer? (Write freely here—thoughts, impressions, scriptures, images, or feelings.)

_____
_____
_____
_____
_____

My "I Will" Statement:

How will I respond to this encounter with God's word? Whom can I share this with today?

_____
_____

| Psalm 140:6-7 | *I say to the LORD, "You are my God." Hear, LORD, my cry for mercy. Sovereign LORD, my strong deliverer, you shield my head in the day of battle.* |

Breath Prayer:

Begin with three slow, deep breaths. Pause briefly between each one. Then, for the next few minutes, prayerfully meditate on these phrases as you breathe:

- Inhale: *"Hear my cry for mercy"*
- Exhale: *"and shield me in times of battle."*

Listening Prayer:

I quiet my heart, turn my attention to Jesus, and simply listen. *What is God speaking to me through this Psalm and this time of meditation?*

Journal Reflection:

What did I sense during my breath or listening prayer? (Write freely here—thoughts, impressions, scriptures, images, or feelings.)

_____

_____

_____

_____

My "I Will" Statement:

How will I respond to this encounter with God's word? Whom can I share this with today?

_____

_____

Psalm 141:1-2

I call to you, LORD, come quickly to me; hear me when I call to you. May my prayer be set before you like incense; may the lifting up of my hands be like the evening sacrifice.

Breath Prayer:

Begin with three slow, deep breaths. Pause briefly between each one. Then, for the next few minutes, prayerfully meditate on these phrases as you breathe:

- Inhale: *"May my prayer be set before you"*
- Exhale: *"like a sweet-smelling sacrifice."*

Listening Prayer:

I quiet my heart, turn my attention to Jesus, and simply listen. *What is God speaking to me through this Psalm and this time of meditation?*

Journal Reflection:

What did I sense during my breath or listening prayer? (Write freely here—thoughts, impressions, scriptures, images, or feelings.)

_____

_____

_____

_____

_____

My "I Will" Statement:

How will I respond to this encounter with God's word? Whom can I share this with today?

_____

_____

> **Psalm 142:1-3**
>
> *I cry aloud to the LORD; I lift up my voice to the LORD for mercy. I pour out before him my complaint; before him I tell my trouble. When my spirit grows faint within me, it is you who watch over my way. In the path where I walk people have hidden a snare for me.*

Breath Prayer:

Begin with three slow, deep breaths. Pause briefly between each one. Then, for the next few minutes, prayerfully meditate on these phrases as you breathe:

- Inhale: *"When my spirit grows faint,"*
- Exhale: *"you watch over my way."*

Listening Prayer:

I quiet my heart, turn my attention to Jesus, and simply listen. *What is God speaking to me through this Psalm and this time of meditation?*

Journal Reflection:

What did I sense during my breath or listening prayer? (Write freely here—thoughts, impressions, scriptures, images, or feelings.)

_____

_____

_____

_____

_____

My "I Will" Statement:

How will I respond to this encounter with God's word? Whom can I share this with today?

_____

_____

Psalm 143:7-8

Answer me quickly, LORD; my spirit fails. Do not hide your face from me or I will be like those who go down to the pit. Let the morning bring me word of your unfailing love, for I have put my trust in you. Show me the way I should go, for to you I entrust my life.

Breath Prayer:

Begin with three slow, deep breaths. Pause briefly between each one. Then, for the next few minutes, prayerfully meditate on these phrases as you breathe:

- Inhale: *"Show me the way I should go,"*
- Exhale: *"for to you I entrust my life."*

Listening Prayer:

I quiet my heart, turn my attention to Jesus, and simply listen. *What is God speaking to me through this Psalm and this time of meditation?*

Journal Reflection:

What did I sense during my breath or listening prayer? (Write freely here—thoughts, impressions, scriptures, images, or feelings.)

_____
_____
_____
_____
_____

My "I Will" Statement:

How will I respond to this encounter with God's word? Whom can I share this with today?

_____
_____

Psalm 144:1-2	*Praise be to the LORD my Rock, who trains my hands for war, my fingers for battle. He is my loving God and my fortress, my stronghold and my deliverer, my shield, in whom I take refuge, who subdues peoples under me.*

Breath Prayer:

Begin with three slow, deep breaths. Pause briefly between each one. Then, for the next few minutes, prayerfully meditate on these phrases as you breathe:

- Inhale: *"You are my Rock and loving God,"*
- Exhale: *"in whom I take refuge."*

Listening Prayer:

I quiet my heart, turn my attention to Jesus, and simply listen. *What is God speaking to me through this Psalm and this time of meditation?*

Journal Reflection:

What did I sense during my breath or listening prayer? (Write freely here—thoughts, impressions, scriptures, images, or feelings.)

_____
_____
_____
_____
_____

My "I Will" Statement:

How will I respond to this encounter with God's word? Whom can I share this with today?

_____
_____

> **Psalm 145:3-5**
>
> *Great is the LORD and most worthy of praise; his greatness no one can fathom. One generation commends your works to another; they tell of your mighty acts. They speak of the glorious splendor of your majesty—and I will meditate on your wonderful works.*

Breath Prayer:

Begin with three slow, deep breaths. Pause briefly between each one. Then, for the next few minutes, prayerfully meditate on these phrases as you breathe:

- Inhale: *"You are great and most worthy of praise."*
- Exhale: *"Your greatness no one can fathom."*

Listening Prayer:

I quiet my heart, turn my attention to Jesus, and simply listen. *What is God speaking to me through this Psalm and this time of meditation?*

Journal Reflection:

What did I sense during my breath or listening prayer? (Write freely here—thoughts, impressions, scriptures, images, or feelings.)

_____
_____
_____
_____

My "I Will" Statement:

How will I respond to this encounter with God's word? Whom can I share this with today?

_____
_____

Psalm 146:1-2

Praise the LORD. Praise the LORD, my soul. I will praise the LORD all my life; I will sing praise to my God as long as I live.

Breath Prayer:

Begin with three slow, deep breaths. Pause briefly between each one. Then, for the next few minutes, prayerfully meditate on these phrases as you breathe:

- Inhale: *"I will offer praise to you, God,"*
- Exhale: *"as long as I live."*

Listening Prayer:

I quiet my heart, turn my attention to Jesus, and simply listen. *What is God speaking to me through this Psalm and this time of meditation?*

Journal Reflection:

What did I sense during my breath or listening prayer? (Write freely here—thoughts, impressions, scriptures, images, or feelings.)

_____

_____

_____

_____

_____

My "I Will" Statement:

How will I respond to this encounter with God's word? Whom can I share this with today?

_____

_____

| **Psalm 147:3-5** | *He heals the brokenhearted and binds up their wounds. He determines the number of the stars and calls them each by name. Great is our Lord and mighty in power; his understanding has no limit.* |

Breath Prayer:

Begin with three slow, deep breaths. Pause briefly between each one. Then, for the next few minutes, prayerfully meditate on these phrases as you breathe:

- Inhale: *"You will heal my broken heart"*
- Exhale: *"and bind up my wounds."*

Listening Prayer:

I quiet my heart, turn my attention to Jesus, and simply listen. *What is God speaking to me through this Psalm and this time of meditation?*

Journal Reflection:

What did I sense during my breath or listening prayer? (Write freely here—thoughts, impressions, scriptures, images, or feelings.)

_____
_____
_____
_____
_____

My "I Will" Statement:

How will I respond to this encounter with God's word? Whom can I share this with today?

_____
_____

Psalm 148:13-14	*Let them praise the name of the LORD, for his name alone is exalted; his splendor is above the earth and the heavens. And he has raised up for his people a horn, the praise of all his faithful servants, of Israel, the people close to his heart. Praise the LORD.*

Breath Prayer:

Begin with three slow, deep breaths. Pause briefly between each one. Then, for the next few minutes, prayerfully meditate on these phrases as you breathe:

- Inhale: *"With all creation, I praise your name,"*
- Exhale: *"for your splendor exceeds it all."*

Listening Prayer:

I quiet my heart, turn my attention to Jesus, and simply listen. *What is God speaking to me through this Psalm and this time of meditation?*

Journal Reflection:

What did I sense during my breath or listening prayer? (Write freely here—thoughts, impressions, scriptures, images, or feelings.)

_____
_____
_____
_____
_____

My "I Will" Statement:

How will I respond to this encounter with God's word? Whom can I share this with today?

_____
_____

| Psalm 149:2-3 | *Let Israel rejoice in their Maker; let the people of Zion be glad in their King. Let them praise his name with dancing and make music to him with timbrel and harp.* |

Breath Prayer:

Begin with three slow, deep breaths. Pause briefly between each one. Then, for the next few minutes, prayerfully meditate on these phrases as you breathe:

- Inhale: *"I rejoice in you, my Maker,"*
- Exhale: *"and am glad that you are my King."*

Listening Prayer:

I quiet my heart, turn my attention to Jesus, and simply listen. *What is God speaking to me through this Psalm and this time of meditation?*

Journal Reflection:

What did I sense during my breath or listening prayer? (Write freely here—thoughts, impressions, scriptures, images, or feelings.)

_____

_____

_____

_____

My "I Will" Statement:

How will I respond to this encounter with God's word? Whom can I share this with today?

_____

_____

Psalm 150:2, 6	*Praise him for his acts of power; praise him for his surpassing greatness. Let everything that has breath praise the LORD. Praise the LORD.*

Breath Prayer:

Begin with three slow, deep breaths. Pause briefly between each one. Then, for the next few minutes, prayerfully meditate on these phrases as you breathe:

- Inhale: *"I praise you for your acts of power"*
- Exhale: *"and for your surpassing greatness."*

Listening Prayer:

I quiet my heart, turn my attention to Jesus, and simply listen. *What is God speaking to me through this Psalm and this time of meditation?*

Journal Reflection:

What did I sense during my breath or listening prayer? (Write freely here—thoughts, impressions, scriptures, images, or feelings.)

_____

_____

_____

_____

_____

My "I Will" Statement:

How will I respond to this encounter with God's word? Whom can I share this with today?

_____

_____

ABOUT THE AUTHOR

Bill and Jill Randall

Over the past 40 years, Bill Randall and his wife, Jill, have followed Jesus with wholehearted devotion, serving across the United States and around the world. Together, they have launched and led numerous churches and missional teams, devoting their lives to equipping and coaching emerging leaders to boldly serve Jesus and advance his Kingdom.

In addition to pioneering new churches, Bill has initiated several Kingdom-focused ventures, including the creation of a ministry leadership degree program at a university, a spiritual formation retreat ministry, and a unique equipping school that prepared ordinary believers for significant leadership roles in and outside of the church.

Since 2014, Bill and Jill have served full-time with **Novo Mission**, a global community of catalytic missionaries dedicated to multiplying gospel movements and mobilizing the Church for mission. As a Vice President of

Novo, Bill founded and leads the **Gospel Movement Teams** division. The global teams he oversees focus on multiplying new disciples of Jesus, new leaders, and new expressions of church in some of the world's most spiritually challenging environments.

Bill's ministry is fueled by a deep passion for abiding with God and helping others cultivate lives of faithfulness and fruitfulness. His work is rooted in scripture, shaped by prayer, and empowered by the Holy Spirit.

He holds an earned doctorate from Fuller Theological Seminary and authored the book, *The Life Jesus Made Possible: Embracing the Kingdom Within Our Reach*, a compelling invitation to live the abundant life Jesus offers.

Bill and Jill reside in Boise, Idaho, enjoying the gift of living near their children and grandchildren. They continue to live out their calling to see the world awakened to the love, truth, and power of Jesus Christ.

Be on the lookout for more books in this Breath Prayers series from Bill!

www.ingramcontent.com/pod-product-compliance
Lightning Source LLC
Chambersburg PA
CBHW071315060426

42444CB00036B/2777